THE NEW DEAL

THE NEW DEAL

What Was It?

Edited by MORTON KELLER

Brandeis University

HOLT, RINEHART AND WINSTON
New York • Chicago • San Francisco • Toronto • London

Cover illustration: Franklin Delano Roosevelt at
Warm Springs, Georgia, December 1, 1933. *(Franklin
D. Roosevelt Library, Hyde Park, New York)*

CONTENTS

INTRODUCTION

At the beginning of the 1930s the American people suffered the most disastrous economic collapse in their history. Theirs was not a unique experience; hard times were shared by most of the Western world. But the stark realities of the Great Depression—widespread poverty in the land of plenty, frustration and despair in the land of opportunity—posed a basic challenge to Americans. Could an open, democratic society survive a major economic collapse and repair the most serious defects of its economic and social structures without a substantial loss of freedom?

It was within the context of this overriding issue that there occurred the outburst of political leadership and legislation, of socioeconomic experimentation and change, that is called the New Deal. The flood of laws, government action, and social planning after 1932 did several basic things: it established the precedent of continuous governmental responsibility for the wellbeing of the economy; it instituted broad social welfare programs; and it worked major shifts in national political allegiances. These were not ephemeral changes, but persist to the present day. Thus any understanding of contemporary America rests heavily on the answer to the question: What was the New Deal?

A proper starting point in the attempt to answer that question is an evaluation of the presidential leadership of Franklin Delano Roosevelt. What were the strengths and weaknesses of that leadership? Was it creative and responsible, or was it a superficial or even a dangerous exercise of presidential power? Was Roosevelt the progenitor—for better or worse—of broad social change? Or was he a temporizer, a compromiser? What, finally, was the most significant of the many roles that he played?

One view sees him as a major figure of the twentieth century: as the man who saved American democracy from the peril of depression and Western democracy from the threat of fascism. Isaiah Berlin's "Roosevelt through European Eyes" is an English expression of this viewpoint. FDR's leadership was for him the determinant that made the New Deal the most hopeful democratic alternative to Fascist or Communist totalitarianism.

Others have offered more equivocal answers to the questions of the nature and significance of Roosevelt's leadership. Daniel Boorstin, in "Selling the President to the People," examines FDR's impact on the institution of the Presidency. He agrees with Berlin that Roosevelt played a role of great im-

1

portance as Chief Executive. But he examines the form of FDR's leadership—the use of mass media, the fabrication and manipulation of public opinion—rather than its content (the theme of Berlin's analysis), and concludes that it substantially furthered certain implicit threats to the proper functioning of the Presidency in the American democratic system.

Richard Hofstadter, discussing "The Roosevelt Reputation," arrives at conclusions strikingly different from the previous selections. Unlike Berlin, he minimizes FDR's role as an outstanding leader of American democracy and stresses instead the highly temporizing, often devious manner of the President's performance. And he differs from both Berlin and Boorstin in finding no great long-run significance in Roosevelt's tenure of office, concluding that FDR by the very nature of his leadership left little in the way of a lasting political heritage.

But the New Deal as an historical phenomenon involved far more than the question of Roosevelt's leadership. Never before in American history had so much new legislation, and legislation of such importance, been passed in so short a time. Never before—save in wartime—had the activities of government such profound and far-reaching consequences for the way of life of the American people. At the time, and since, attempts have been made to assess the significance of the New Deal's policies. Did these policies amount to an alien, dangerous revolution in American political, economic, and social patterns? Or were they a more or less successful sequence of responses to the problems posed by the Great Depression, responses standing well within the American reform tradition? Did they add up to an orderly, purposeful program? Or were they contradictory and/or ineffective policies?

What is commonly called the First New Deal included attempts to restore America's economic vitality and reform her stricken economic institutions, and efforts for relief and reform which were directed more toward people than toward institutions. What caused so sudden and so extensive a body of laws? What common elements, if any, bound together these diverse enactments? These problems are the underlying concerns of the selections from Basil Rauch's *The History of the New Deal* and Edgar E. Robinson's *The Roosevelt Leadership*.

Rauch's discussion of the development of the First New Deal interprets it as a desirable, democratic program of recovery, relief, and reform, made necessary by the accumulated evils of a business-dominated economy. He argues that the measures for social relief and reform were more significant than the ones for economic recovery; that the major issues of the First New Deal were the attempt of big business to control the National Recovery Administration and the relationship of the Roosevelt administration to the rising demands of labor; and that the unreasonable resistance of the business community helped to bring on the more important and more permanent achievements of the Second New Deal. Thus for Rauch the major force in the early New Deal was the interplay of various interest groups, and the central theme of those years was the Roosevelt administration's growing responsiveness to the aspirations of the most needy of those interests: labor, farmers, small businessmen.

Robinson's view of the developments of 1933 and 1934 is different indeed. While admitting the seriousness of the situation that existed when Roosevelt took office, he argues that FDR soon moved to new and disturbing forms of government action not indicated in his 1932 campaign. The development of the New Deal was not, as Rauch saw it, a response to national conditions and popular demands so much as it was the work of administration officials influenced by alien and socialistic ideas who without any popular mandate sought to recast American society.

From 1935 to 1938 a second wave of legislation—a Second New Deal—appeared, concentrating not so much on the recovery and rehabilitation of the economic structure as on further attempts at social relief and reform. Raymond Moley's "Lost Directions" and the *New Republic* editors' "New Deal in Review" seek to cope with the problems raised by the Second New Deal: What were its sources? What were its purposes? What were its consequences?

Moley, an important adviser to Franklin Roosevelt during the early days of the New Deal, found the spirit of the later years alarming. He was especially disturbed by what he took to be FDR's increasing fondness for the powers of the Presidency and increasing willingness to see himself as one at war with the American business community. Comparing the earlier and later New Deals, Moley concluded that there were no consistent, no unifying purposes, and that in the last analysis the prime force directing the evolution of the New Deal was the growing demagoguery and desire for power of FDR and his later advisers.

The editors of the *New Republic,* examining the Second New Deal in 1940, came to very different conclusions as to its purposes and effects. Their primary criticism of the later New Deal was precisely the opposite of Moley's: that it was overly friendly, not overly hostile, toward big business. And while Moley identified Roosevelt's pride and ambition as the source of the New Deal's development, the *New Republic* selection stressed instead the administration's increasingly sensitive response to the social ills of American life.

The Rauch, Robinson, Moley, and *New Republic* selections, each analyzing in its own way a period of the New Deal's evolution, have in common their concern with a central problem: Why did the New Deal develop as it did? Why did an administration initially dedicated to the specific purpose of battling the Great Depression expand into one of American history's major periods of governmental innovation? Rauch and the editors of the *New Repub-*

lic, observers sympathetic to the New Deal, attribute its evolution to the intense and widespread popular demand for the reform of a society whose political system, economic institutions, and social structure had been dominated for too long by business interests. Robinson and Moley, equally committed in their hostility to the New Deal's development, center their analyses on its inner workings rather than its external pressures, that is to say, on the aspirations of FDR's advisers and the ambitions of FDR himself.

World War II and the "cold war" brought substantial prosperity to most Americans, and the thrust of the New Deal all but disappeared. Yet its legislation has remained, never seriously challenged. Attempts to explain what the New Deal was, and what impact it has had on American life, continue unabated.

With the passage of time interpretations of the New Deal tend increasingly to treat it as a complete historical phenomenon, whose beginnings, development, and end are of a piece. Special attention has been paid to the problem of its origins, and to the place it occupies in the long-range perspective of American history. What gave it birth? What forces fed its development? What effect has it had on American society? These are the problems that, to varying degrees, are dealt with in the selections interpreting the New Deal as an historical event.

FDR himself helped to set the tone for one overview of the New Deal when he described it in 1934 as "a satisfactory combination of the Square Deal and the New Freedom ... the fulfilment of the progressive ideas expounded by Theodore Roosevelt of a partnership between business and government and also of the determination of Woodrow Wilson that business should be subjected, through the power of government, to drastic legal limitations against abuses." Rexford G. Tugwell, a prominent figure in the later Roosevelt administration, sees "The New Deal in Retrospect" very much in these terms: as the culmination of a reform era stretching back to the beginning of the twentieth century. Far from marking a revolutionary change in American life, argues Tugwell, the New Deal may well have been only "a progressive interlude in an America predominantly reactionary."

Two other selections—Charles A. Beard and George H. E. Smith's "An Epitome of Characteristics," and Benjamin Stolberg and Warren Jay Vinton's "Roosevelt Panaceas"—agree on the nonrevolutionary character of the New Deal. But they do not share Tugwell's conviction that it was a successful movement of reform. Beard and Smith criticize the New Deal for preserving all too many of the defects of the past. Much more caustically, Stolberg and Vinton condemn it as a superficial, inconsistent effort at reform that failed to come to grips with the fundamental issues of American capitalism, that, indeed, tended to protect and preserve all too many of those evils.

Another analytical theme stresses the uniqueness of the New Deal, **its** break with past reform movements, and the substantial—even revolutionary—changes it wrought in American life. Arthur M. Schlesinger, Jr's "Sources of the New Deal" examines the tensions and discontents of the 1920s, and the widespread frustration and despair that came to the Western world with the Great Depression of the 1930s. These he considers to have been the circumstances that gave the New Deal its special spirit and direction.

Amaury de Riencourt's *The Coming Caesars* echoes Schlesinger's view that the New Deal came at a time of crisis in the Western world, but he argues that the movement was a symptom of the malaise, not its potential cure. He equates the New Deal with the Caesarism of ancient Rome and judges it to be a milder, American equivalent of the drift to totalitarianism prevalent in twentieth century Europe.

Samuel Lubell in "The Revolt of the City" shares with Schlesinger and Riencourt a sense of the essential novelty of the New Deal, but finds its major source in yet another set of conditions. It was a fresh force in American history, he argues, because the Roosevelt administration came to voice the aspirations of voters—urban, lower-income, often ethnic minority (Catholic, Negro, Jewish)—who traditionally had had little representation in American politics. While Schlesinger and Riencourt treat the New Deal primarily as an ideological phenomenon, Lubell see it as a political expression of certain fundamental changes in the nature of the American population.

Thus explanations of where the New Deal came from, what it was, and what its effects have been, exist in abundance. To a great extent, writings on the movement are still caught up in the passions of the time, and a mature historical perspective is very difficult to attain. But the reader of the selections that follow may come reasonably close to such a perspective if he seeks out answers to these questions:

What was Franklin D. Roosevelt's relationship to the New Deal: was he truly a leader who for better or worse shaped the New Deal to his wishes, or was he a political manipulator without any real sense of purpose? If he did have a sense of purpose, was it primarily dedicated to changing important areas of American life, or to restraining stronger forces for change?

Why did the New Deal develop as it did? What factors gave it its initial form; what changed that form; what brought the evolution of the New Deal to an end?

What was the relationship of the New Deal to other American political movements, to the American society of its time? What have been the effects of the New Deal on American life since: what aspects seem to have been only temporary, and what seems to be permanent?

Such questions will not soon have their definitive answers. But they will be asked again and again as succeeding generations seek to explain, in terms satisfactory to themselves, the historical phenomenon of the New Deal.

THE CLASH OF CONTEMPORARIES

(In 1938 the editors of *Time* invited their readers to define the New Deal. These are some of the replies.)

Define the New Deal? Tammany methods made magnificent.

... I wish to submit the essence of three schools of thought as to the meaning of the term:

1. *Left-Wing opinion.* The New Deal was designed by Franklin D. Roosevelt, a millionaire political demagogue, for the purpose of prolonging the life of the archaic and defunct capitalistic system....

2. *New Deal opinion.* The New Deal is the name given to F. D. Roosevelt's political, social and economic program which has for its aim the conservation of America's human and natural resources, guided by the principle of the "greatest good to the greatest number"....

3. *Right-Wing opinion.* The New Deal is the ambiguous label of Roosevelt II's multifarious, opportunistic, meddlesome, extravagant, pseudo-social, alphabetical agencies designed to make this country safe for the Democratic party....

... In the heat of the presidential campaign of 1936, the local Democratic headquarters received a telephone call. "Say," a voice exclaimed, "tell us just what the principles of the New Deal are—we're having an argument." "Hold the phone," was the answering injunction, followed by a long pause. Then: "Sorry. We're having an argument, too."

Perhaps the New Deal might be defined as bewildered idealism, leftish in objectives, rightish in methods, misunderstood by liberals, misused by conservatives, mistrusted by businessmen—but still relied upon reluctantly by indebted farmers, doubtfully by organized labor, helplessly by the unemployed, and hopefully by bewildered idealists.

The New Deal: a courageous attempt to remake America overnight, doomed to failure because Americans cannot adapt themselves so quickly; an attempt right in principle and aim, wrong in numberless details....

... Yesterday we used the word reform.

SIR ISAIAH BERLIN (1909–   ), Chichele Professor
of Social and Political Theory at All Souls
College, Oxford, has an international reputation
as a philosopher and historian. The following selection,
from an address originally delivered over the British
Broadcasting Corporation on the tenth anniversary
of FDR's death, eloquently reveals the impact that
the American President had on most liberals and
intellectuals in the Western world. As a European,
Sir Isaiah dwells on the international implications of
Roosevelt's domestic and foreign policies.*

Roosevelt through European Eyes

... When I say that some men occupy one's imagination for many years, this is literally true of Mr. Roosevelt's effect on the young men of my own generation in England, and probably in many parts of Europe, and indeed the entire world. If one was young in the thirties and lived in a democracy, then, whatever one's politics, if one had human feelings at all, or the faintest spark of social idealism, or any love of life, one must have felt very much as young men in Continental Europe probably felt after the defeat of Napoleon during the years of the Restoration: that all was dark and quiet, a great reaction was abroad, and little stirred, and nothing resisted. . . .

The most insistent propaganda in those days declared that humanitarianism and liberalism and democratic forces were played out, and that the choice now lay between two bleak extremes, Communism and Fascism—the red or the black. To those who were not carried away by this patter the only light in the darkness was the administration of Mr. Roosevelt and the New Deal in the United States. At a time of weakness and mounting despair in the democratic world, Mr. Roosevelt radiated confidence and strength. He was the leader of the democratic world, and even today upon him alone, of all the statesmen of the thirties, no cloud has rested—neither on him nor on the New Deal, which to European eyes still looks a bright chapter in the history of

* Isaiah Berlin, "Roosevelt through European Eyes," *Atlantic Monthly,* vol. 196 (July 1955), pp. 67–71.

mankind. It was true that his great social experiment was conducted with an isolationist disregard of the outside world, but it was psychologically intelligible that America, which had come into being in reaction against the follies and evils of a Europe perpetually distraught by religious or national struggles, should try to seek salvation undisturbed by the currents of European life, particularly at a moment when Europe seemed about to collapse into a totalitarian nightmare. . . .

His internal policy was plainly animated by a humanitarian purpose. After the unbridled individualism of the twenties which had led to economic collapse and widespread misery, he was seeking to establish new rules of social justice. He was trying to do this without forcing his country into some doctrinaire strait jacket, whether of socialism or state capitalism or the kind of new social organization which the Fascist régimes flaunted as the New Order. Social discontent was high in the United States; faith in businessmen as saviors of society had evaporated overnight after the famous Wall Street crash, and Mr. Roosevelt was providing a vast safety valve for pent-up bitterness and indignation, and trying to prevent revolution and construct a régime which should establish greater economic equality, social justice and happiness, above all, human happiness—ideals which were in the best tradition of American life—without altering the basis of freedom and democracy in his country.

This was being done by what, to unsympathetic critics, seemed a haphazard collection of amateurs, college professors, journalists, personal friends, free lances of one kind or another, intellectuals, ideologists—what are nowadays called eggheads—whose very appearance and methods of conducting business or constructing policies irritated the servants of old established government institutions in Washington and tidy-minded conservatives everywhere. Yet it was clear that the very amateurishness of these men, the fact that they were allowed to talk to their hearts' content, to experiment, to indulge in a vast amount of trial and error, that relations were personal and not institutional, bred its own vitality and enthusiasm.

Washington was doubtless full of quarrels, resignations, palace intrigues, perpetual warfare between individuals and groups of individuals, parties, cliques, personal supporters of this or that great captain, which must have maddened sober and responsible officials used to the slower tempo and more normal patterns of administration. As for bankers and businessmen, the feelings of many of them were past describing; but at this period they were little regarded, since they were considered to have discredited themselves too deeply, and indeed forever.

Over this vast, seething chaos presided a handsome, charming, gay, intelligent, delightful, very audacious man, Mr. Franklin Delano Roosevelt. He was accused of many weaknesses. He had betrayed his class; he was ignorant, unscrupulous, irresponsible. He was ruthless in playing with the lives and careers of individuals. He was surrounded by adventurers, slick opportunists, intriguers. He made conflicting promises, cynically and brazenly, to individuals and groups and representatives of foreign nations. He made up, with his vast and irresistible public charm and his astonishing high spirits, for a lack of virtues considered more important in the leader of the most powerful democracy in the world: the virtues of application, industry, responsibility.

All this was said and some of it may indeed have been just. What attracted his followers were countervailing qualities of a rare and inspiring order. He was large-hearted and possessed wide political horizons, imaginative sweep, understanding of the time in which he lived and of the direction of the great new forces at work in the twentieth century—technological, racial, imperialist, anti-imperialist. He was in favor of life and movement, the promotion of the most generous possible fulfillment of the largest possible number of human wishes, and not in favor of caution and retrenchment and sitting still. Above all, he was absolutely fearless.

He was one of the few statesmen in the twentieth or any other century who seemed to have no fear at all of the future. He believed in his own strength and ability to manage, and to succeed, whatever happened. He believed in the capacity and loyalty of his lieutenants, so that he looked upon the future with a calm eye, as if to say, "Let it come, whatever it may be, it will all be grist to our great mill. We shall turn it all to benefit." It was this, perhaps, more than any other quality, which drew men of very different outlooks to him. In a despondent world which appeared divided between wicked and fatally efficient fanatics marching to destroy, and bewildered populations on the run, unenthusiastic martyrs in a cause they could not define, he believed in his own ability, so long as he was in control, to stem the terrible tide.

He had all the character and energy and skill of the dictators, and he was on our side. He was, in his opinions and public actions, every inch a democrat.

All the political and personal and public criticism of him might be true; all the personal defects which his enemies and some of his friends attributed to him might be real; yet as a public figure he was unique. As the skies of Europe grew darker, in particular after war broke out, he seemed to the poor and the unhappy in Europe a kind of benevolent demigod who alone could and would save them in the end. His moral authority, the degree of confidence which he inspired outside his own country—far more beyond America's frontiers than within them at all times—has no parallel. Perhaps President Wilson in the early days after the end of the First World War, when he drove in triumph through the streets of London and Paris, may have inspired some such feeling; but it disappeared quickly and left behind it a terrible feeling of disenchantment. It was plain even to his enemies that President Roosevelt would not be broken as President Wilson had been. For to his prestige and to his personality he added a degree of political skill—indeed virtuosity—which no American before him had ever possessed. His chance of realizing his wishes was plainly greater; his followers would be less likely to reap bitter disappointment....

As I said before, he was, by some of his opponents, accused of betraying his class; and so he had. When a man who retains the manners, style of life, the emotional texture and the charm of the old order, of some free aristocratic upbringing, revolts against his milieu and adopts the ideas and aspirations of the new, socially *révolté* class—and adopts them not from motives of expediency but out of genuine moral conviction, or from love of life—inability to remain on the side of what seems to him narrow, corrupt, mean, restrictive—the result is fascinating and moving. . . . It was this gentlemanly quality, together with the fact that they felt him to be deeply committed to their side in the struggle and in favor of their way of life, as well as his open and fearless lack of neutrality in the war against the Nazis and Fascists, that endeared him so deeply to the British people during the war years.

I remember well in London, in November, 1940, how excited most people were about the result of the presidential election in the United States. In theory they need not have worried. Mr. Willkie, the Republican candidate, had expressed himself forcibly and sincerely as a supporter of the democracies. Yet it was absurd to say that the people of Britain were neutral in their feelings vis-à-vis the two candidates. They felt in their bones that Mr. Roosevelt was their lifelong friend, that he hated the Nazis as deeply as they did, that he wanted democracy and civilization, in the sense in which they believed in it, to prevail, that he knew what he wanted, and that his goal resembled their own ideals more than it did those of all his opponents. They felt that his heart was in the right place, and they did not, therefore, if they gave it a thought, care whether his political appointments were made under the influence of bosses, or for personal reasons, or thoughtlessly; whether his economic doctrines were heretical; whether he had a sufficiently scrupulous regard for the views of the Senate or the House of Representatives, or the prescriptions of the United States Constitution, or the opinions of the Supreme Court. These matters were very remote from them. They knew that he would, to the extent of his enormous energy and ability, see them through.

There is probably no such thing as

long-lived mass hypnotism; the masses know what it is that they like, what genuinely appeals to them. What most Germans thought Hitler to be, Hitler, in fact, largely was; and what free men in Europe and in America and in Asia and in Africa and in Australia, and wherever else the rudiments of free political thought stirred at all—what all these felt Roosevelt to be, he, in fact, was. He was the greatest leader of democracy, the greatest champion of social progress, in the twentieth century.

His enemies accused him of plotting to get America into the war. I am not competent to discuss this controversial issue, but it seems to me that the evidence for it is lacking. I think that when he promised to keep America at peace he meant to try as hard as he could to do so, compatibly with helping to promote the victory of the democracies. He must at one period have thought that he could win the war without entering it, and so, at the end of it, be in the unique position, hitherto achieved by no one, of being the arbiter of the world's fate, without needing to placate those bitter forces which involvement in a war inevitably brings about, and which are an obstacle to reason and humanity in the making of the peace.

No doubt he trusted too often in his own magical power of improvisation. Doubtless he made many political mistakes, some of them difficult to remedy. Some say he was disastrously wrong about Stalin and his intentions and the nature of the Soviet state; others, with equal justice, point to his coolness to the Free French movement, his cavalier intentions with regard to the Supreme Court in the United States, his errors about a good many other issues. He irritated his staunchest supporters and most faithful servants because he did not tell them what he was doing; his government was highly personal and it maddened tidy-minded officials and humiliated those who thought that his policy should be conducted in consultation with and through them. His anti-imperialism at times (in Yalta, for example) assumed gaily irresponsible forms. He vastly oversimplified many issues. He overestimated his own capacity to build a new world by the sole use of his own prodigious powers of manipulation in the course of breezily informal dealings with other statesmen on a purely personal basis. All this sometimes exasperated his allies, but when these last bethought them of who most of his ill-wishers were in the United States and in the world outside, and what *their* motives were, their own respect, affection, and loyalty tended to return. No man made more public enemies, yet no man had a right to take greater pride in the quality and the motives of some of those enemies. He could justly call himself the friend of the people, and although his opponents accused him of being a demagogue, this charge seems to me unjust. He did not sacrifice fundamental political principles to a desire to retain power; he did not whip up evil passions merely in order to avenge himself upon those whom he disliked or wished to crush, or because it was an atmosphere in which he found it convenient to operate. He saw to it that his administration was in the van of public opinion and drew it on instead of being dragged by it. He made the majority of his fellow citizens prouder to be Americans than they had been before. He raised their status in their own eyes, and in those of the rest of the world. It was an extraordinary transformation of an individual. Perhaps it was largely brought about by the collapse of his health in the early twenties, and his marvelous triumph over his disabilities. For he began life as well-born, polite, agreeable, debonair, not particularly gifted young man, something of a prig, liked but not greatly admired by his contemporaries at Groton and at Harvard, a competent Assistant Secretary of the Navy in the First World War; in short, he seemed embarked on the routine career of an American patrician with moderate political ambitions. His illness and the support and encouragement and political qualities of his wife—whose greatness of character and goodness of heart history will duly record—seemed to transfigure his public personality into the strong and beneficient champion who became the father of his people, in an altogether unique fashion.

He was more than this: it is not too much to say that he altered the fundamental concept of government and its obligations to the governed. . . . The welfare state, so much denounced, has obviously come to stay: the direct moral responsibility for minimum standards of living and social services which it took for granted, are today accepted almost without a murmur by the most conservative politicians in the Western democracies. The Republican Party in 1952 made no effort to upset the basic principles—which seemed utopian in the twenties—of Mr. Roosevelt's social legislation.

But Mr. Roosevelt's greatest service to mankind (after ensuring victory against the enemies of freedom) consists in the fact that he showed that it is possible to be politically effective and yet benevolent and civilized: that the fierce left and right wing propaganda of the thirties, according to which the conquest and retention of political power is not compatible with human qualities, but necessarily demands from those who pursue it seriously the sacrifice of their lives upon the altar of some ruthless ideology, or the systematic practice of depotism— this propaganda, which filled the art and talk of the day, was simply untrue. Mr. Roosevelt's example strengthened democracy everywhere—that is to say, the view that the promotion of social justice and individual liberty does not neces-sarily mean the end of all efficient government; that power and order are not identical with a strait jacket of doctrine, whether economic or political; that it is possible to reconcile individual liberty and a loose texture of society with the indispensable minimum of organization and authority. And in this belief lies what Mr. Roosevelt's greatest predecessor once described as the last best hope on earth.

As the New Deal slips deeper into the past, interpretations of FDR set him into a broader historical context. The following essay is by DANIEL J. BOORSTIN (1914–   ), professor of American history at the University of Chicago. He looks at FDR not as a political leader, but as a President who boldly used the media of mass communications and thus enmeshed his office in the web of public relations. Boorstin is one of the post-New Deal generation of American historians who, while fundamentally sympathetic to the movement, look critically at what they consider to be some of its undesirable consequences.*

Selling the President to the People

...FDR was our first "nationally advertised" President. The attitude of the vast majority of the American people to him was as different from that of their grandfathers to the Presidents of their day as our attitude to General Motors is different from that of our great-grandfathers to the village harness-maker. Like other "nationally advertised brands," FDR could not, of course, have been successful if he had not had something to offer. But would he have been able to sell himself to the American public—and on such a scale—without the benefit of certain technological changes in our systems of public communication?...

By the time that Franklin Delano Roosevelt came into office on March 4, 1933, technological and institutional innovations had in many ways prepared the way for a transformation of the relation between President and people. Communications from the President to the reading or listening public, which formerly had been ceremonial, infrequent, and addressed to small audiences, could now be constant, spontaneous, and directed to all who could read or hear (sometimes whether they wished to or not). And now through the questions put to the President at his regular press conferences, and through the telegrams and mail received after his radio addresses or public statements, he could sense the temper and gauge the drift of public opinion—he could find out what the sovereign people wanted. He could even send up trial balloons to get some advance

* Daniel J. Boorstin, "Selling the President to the People," *Commentary*, vol. 20 (November 1955), pp. 421–424. This article is also found in Boorstin, *America and the Image of Europe* (Meridian Books, Inc., 1960).

idea of public response to his future decisions. The President was no longer simply dealing with the "people," but with "public opinion."

There is no denying that FDR possessed a genius for using these new means of communication. Without them he could hardly have developed that novel intimacy between people and President which marked his administrations. In the little memorial miscellany published by Pocket Books on April 18, 1945 (less than a week after FDR's death), we read in Carl Carmer's verse dialogue:

Woman:
. . . Come home with me
If you would think of him. I never saw him—
But I knew him. Can you have forgotten
How, with his voice, he came into our house,
The President of these United States,
Calling us friends. . . .
Do you remember how he came to us
That day twelve years ago—a little more—
And you were sitting by the radio
(We had it on the kitchen table then)
Your head down on your arms as if asleep.

For the first time in American history the voice of the President was a voice from kitchen tables, from the counters of bars and lunchrooms, and the corners of living rooms.

FDR's relaxed and informal style, both in writing and speaking, enabled him to make the most of the new informal circumstances under which people heard him. That he was compelled by his infirmity to sit while giving his radio talks only added to the informality. A whole world separates FDR's speeches from those of his immediate predecessors —from the stilted rhetoric of the oratory collected in such volumes as Calvin Coolidge's *Foundations of the Republic* (1926) or Herbert Hoover's *Addresses Upon the American Road* (1938). Earlier

Presidential speeches had too often echoed the style and sentiments of commencement addresses; FDR could say something informal and concrete even in such an unpromising State Paper as a "Mother's Day Proclamation."

Perhaps never before had there been so happy a coincidence of personal talent with technological opportunity as under his administrations. In the eight volumes of the *Public Papers and Addresses of Franklin D. Roosevelt,* which cover the era of the New Deal, we discover two new genres of political literature which were the means by which a new relationship between President and people was fashioned. The first genre was established in transcriptions of Presidential press conferences; the second, in FDR's radio talks, the "fireside chats." Both are distinguished by an engaging casualness and directness; but this is not all that makes them new genres in the literature of American politics. Here, for the first time among Presidential papers, we find an extensive body of public utterances that are unceremonial yet serious.

Only a year after FDR assumed office, Theodore G. Joslin, who had handled press relations for President Hoover, observed that President Roosevelt had already come nearer than any of his predecessors "to meeting the expectations of the four hundred men and women who, in these times of stress, write half a million words a day to bring to our firesides news of developments at the seat of the Government." FDR had already shown the cameraderie and the willingness to make news which made some correspondents (not always his political friends) call his administration a "new deal for the press." The unprecedented frequency of his press conferences established a continuity of relations with both correspondents and the reading public. During Hoover's administration there had been only sixty-six Presidential press conferences; but FDR held three hundred thirty-seven press conferences during his first administration, and three hundred seventy-four during his second. Thus, while Hoover met the press on an average of less than once in every three weeks, Roosevelt would see them about five times in that same period. The record of his conferences shows how this frequency bred intimacy, informality, and a set of institutionalized procedures; before long the spirit of those press conferences became on both sides much like that of any other responsible deliberative body.

Similarly, the frequency with which the President went on the air effected a revolutionary change. Between March and October 1933, FDR gave four "fireside chats." Through these, for the first time in American history, a President was able to appeal on short notice and in his own voice to the whole constituency. Neither the press conference nor the "fireside chat" was an occasion for *ex cathedra* pronouncements. On the contrary, they were designed to stimulate a more active "dialogue" between the people and the Chief Executive.

Perhaps the best index of the effect of FDR's radio talks was the volume of White House mail. In McKinley's time Presidential mail amounted to about a hundred letters a day, which were handled by a single clerk. Despite occasional flurries at inaugurations or crises, the daily flow remained small. Not until President Hoover's time did its volume increase significantly. Even then letters sometimes did not number more than a few hundred a day, and the system of handling them remained unchanged. Under FDR, however, Presidential mail acquired a new and unprecedented volume, as we learn from the reminiscences of Ira R. T. Smith, for many years chief Presidential mail clerk (*"Dear Mr. President...": The Story of Fifty Years in the White House Mail Room*):

Mr. Roosevelt always showed a keen interest in the mail and kept close watch on its trend. Nothing pleased him more than to know that I had to build up a big staff and often had to work until midnight to keep up with a run of 5000 to 8000 letters a day, and on some occasions many more thousands. He received regular reports.... Whenever there was a decrease in the influx of letters we could expect to hear from him or one of his secretaries, who wanted to know what was the matter—was the President losing his grip on the public?

Before FDR came to the White House, Mr. Smith had handled all the mail by himself. But when, in response to his First Inaugural Address, FDR received over four hundred fifty thousand letters, it was plain that a new era had begun. During certain periods as many as fifty persons were required to open and sort the White House mail; before long an electric letter-opener was installed, and instead of the old practice of counting individual pieces of mail, Mr. Smith and his helpers began measuring stacked-up letters by the yard.

Also, a new self-consciousness governed FDR's communications to the public; the era of "public relations" had begun. It was enough that the President (or someone else for him) should state what he really believed—one had to consider all the "angles." Andrew Jackson had had his Amos Kendall and his Frank Blair; and it had not been uncommon for Presidents to employ ghost writers and close personal advisers who, in some cases, were responsible for both style and content. But perhaps never before did a President depend so consistently and to such an extent in his literary product on the collaboration of advisers. Among FDR's speech-writers were men like Harry Hopkins, Robert Sherwood, Samuel Rosenman, Stanley High, Charles Michelson, Ernest Lindley, Sumner Welles, Raymond Moley, Rexford Tugwell, Archibald MacLeish, Tom Corcoran, Basil O'Connor, and Robert Jackson—and these are only a few. FDR's speeches, even the most important and those seemingly most personal, were as much a cooperative product as a piece of copy produced by a large advertising agency. The President's genius consisted very much in his ability to give calculated, pre-fabricated phrases an air of casualness. It was, of course, remarkable that his speeches retained any personal flavor at all. And it was significant that this collaborative literary activity was not kept secret. The public began to take it as much for granted that the utterances of a President should be a composite product as that an advertisement of the Ford Motor Company should not be written by Henry Ford.

In the longer perspective of American history, these changes that FDR, aided by technology, brought about in the conduct of the Presidency may become permanent and take on the quality of mutations:

1. *The decline in the periodicity of American political life.* In the early years of the Republic, politics—or at least national politics—was a "sometime thing." Political interest would rise to fever pitch before national elections or in times of crisis, and tend to subside in between. The very vastness of the country reinforced this tendency to periodicity in American political life. And so our elections became notorious for their barbecue, holiday atmosphere: brief but hectic interruptions of the routines of life.

But the technological developments which I have described increased the President's opportunity, and eventually his need, to make news. Now headlines could be produced at an hour's notice. To oblige the correspondents by making big stories frequently, and small stories constantly, became part of his job. In FDR's era, of course, the crises in economic life and international affairs were themselves rich raw material for the press. There had been crises and wars before, but never before had so large and steady a stream of announcements, information, "statements to the press," and description of "problems facing the country" poured from the headquarters of government. The innocent citizen now found no respite from this barrage of politics and government. Even over a beer at his favorite bar he was likely to hear the hourly news broadcast, or the very voice of his President.

The citizen was no longer expected to focus his attention only temporarily on a cluster of issues (conveniently dramatized by two rival personalities) at the time of national election. With the rise of the weekly news magazine (*Time* was founded in 1923, *Newsweek* in 1938), of news quizzes, news broadcasts, and radio forums, the citizen was given a new duty, that of being "well informed." The complex of alphabetical agencies, the intricate and remote problems of foreign policy, and the details of the legislative process came now, as never before, to burden his mind and plague his conscience. Whether or not the American citizen was consciously becoming more "political," he was surely finding it more and more difficult to escape politics. No longer was he granted the surcease of inter-election periods when his representatives were left to their own devices and he could turn to other things. Paradoxically, in spite of the great increase in population, the national government was becoming less and less republican, and more and more democratic; for elected officials were now in more constant touch with their constituencies.

2. *Increased communication between the people and the President.* The very agencies that the President was now using to communicate his views to the public were also employed to elicit the public's response. Letters to the President—and to Congressmen—became a special American version of the ancient right of petition. As communications to public officials multiplied, the temptations increased for the public official, and especially the President, to trim his sails to the shifting winds of opinion, which now sometimes blew with hurricane force into Washington offices. The weak representative or the demagogue would find it easier to be weak and yet to seem to be strong by following the majority view at every turn. Here was still another force to prevent the realization of Burke's ideal of the independent representative, and to make him a "mere" spokesman of popular views.

3. *The decline of naivety.* The efflorescence of "public relations" techniques and of opinion polls increased the temptation for the President to rely on experts in dealing with the public. Even if Presidential utterances would still have the appearance of casualness, it would be a studied casualness, or one that the people would suspect of being studied.

The President would scrutinize surveys of press opinions; he would employ (sometimes within the very agencies of government) specialists in "opinion research" to inform him of what the people liked or disliked. In these ways, the citizen was more and more assimilated to the customer; he had to be "approached," his responses had to be measured so that he could be given what he wanted, or thought he wanted.

4. *The inversion of geographic and political distances.* The new developments in communications made many of the oldest assumptions about the relations between geography and politics irrelevant. Jefferson and his "States Rights" disciples had started from the axiom that the citizen's knowledge and hence his capacity for an informed opinion were in inverse ratio to his geographic distance from the headquarters of decision. The closer he was to the scene, the more he would presumably know, and the more exact would be his knowledge. Thus the average citizen was expected to be best informed about the political affairs of his municipality, only a little less informed about those of his state, and considerably less informed about the affairs of the nation as a whole. The changes that reached their climax under FDR not only exploded this assumption, they came close to making it the reverse of the truth. Both the multiplication of newscasts and the expansion of the profession of radio news-commentator focused attention on national events—since these were sure to interest the largest number of listeners; and audience volume decided where money was to be invested in communications. National affairs became more and more a good thing for the commercial sponsors of newscasts. Inevitably, many of the ablest

reporters, too, were attracted to the national capital. The citizen, when he listened to the news from Washington, now had the benefit of sophisticated, well-informed, and competent interpreters who seldom had equals in the state capitals or on the local scene.

There thus developed a new disparity between the quality and quantity of information about national as contrasted with state or local matters. By about 1940, largely owing to the press and the radio, the citizenry had clearly reached a point where it was better informed about national than about local issues. This reversal of a long-standing assumption, which was not just a result of the marked increase in federal activities under the New Deal, would require revision of accepted notions about federalism, and about the competence of the average citizen to participate in government.

We are already far enough from the age of FDR to begin to see that the tendencies which I have just described were not ephemeral. American experience under FDR created new expectations that continue to clamor for fulfillment.

When we look on into the administrations of Truman and Eisenhower, we see that these expectations became institutionalized. FDR had set a style that later Presidential candidates could only at their peril violate. President Truman's success and the defeat of Governor Dewey in the 1948 elections cannot be explained unless such novel factors are taken into account. The growth of television, and its frequent (and on the whole successful) use by President Eisenhower, only carry further the tendencies initiated in the age of FDR. While later Presidents might lack the vividness of FDR's personality, perhaps never again would any man attain the Presidency or discharge its duties satisfactorily without entering into an intimate and conscious relation with the whole public. This opens unprecedented opportunities for effective and enlightening leadership. But it also opens unprecedented temptations. For never before has it been so easy for a statesman to seem to lead millions while in reality tamely echoing their every shifting mood and inclination.

RICHARD HOFSTADTER (1916–   ), De Witt
Clinton Professor of American History at Columbia
University, is in the first rank of contemporary
American historians. The following selection is in
the spirit of his book *The American Political
Tradition and the Men Who Made It* (New York,
1949), which took a critical look at American political
history as a succession of essentially similar, essentially
unsatisfactory compromises. Like Boorstin, Hofstadter
wrote in the atmosphere of disenchantment with the
New Deal that was prevalent in the years immediately
after FDR's death. In a later book, *The Age of Reform*
(New York, 1955), Hofstadter concludes that
Roosevelt's New Deal was more original and productive
than he had previously thought.*

The Roosevelt Reputation

The public reputation of a political
hero is a political and ideological fact
of the greatest importance, a major clue
to the state of the national mind. The
current battle over the reputation of
Franklin D. Roosevelt provides one symptom of a continuing ideological struggle
which began with the Great Depression,
a struggle of which we are only beginning to gain perspective. The revelations
made during the past two years by Roosevelt's friends and associates—Frances Perkins, Cordell Hull, James A. Farley,
Harry Hopkins, Henry Morgenthau, Jr.,
John Garner, Ed Flynn, and Henry L.
Stimson—have the combined effect, although some intend to praise and others
to criticize, of cutting him down to size,

of providing us with some preliminary
measure of the gap between Roosevelt
the myth and Roosevelt the man.

If anyone ever had the notion that
the New Deal insiders made one big
happy family, with F.D.R. as the beloved
and venerated father, that notion will
certainly be dissipated by looking into
Cordell Hull's memoirs, *Jim Farley's
Story*, and the recollections of John
Garner. Both Hopkins' and Morgenthau's reports, although written from an
admiring standpoint, contain material
which could as well be used by Roosevelt's critics as his admirers. And what
has thus far been published from the
Morgenthau diaries contains a kind of
unintentional self-criticism which may

---

* Richard Hofstadter, "The Roosevelt Reputation," *The Progressive*, vol. 12 (November 1948), pp. 9–12.

cause many people to ponder the principles governing Roosevelt's choice of associates.

The late President now appears in several perspectives: as a facile, egotistical, and evasive prima donna (Farley, Garner, Hull), a warm and sympathetic, although fallible friend (Perkins), as a great world leader struggling against many grave handicaps (Stimson), and as a resolute and tireless practical idealist (Hopkins).

It has long been recognized that the New Deal was an incongruous alliance of unlike interests—of conservative Southern Democrats and almost equally conservative Northern city machines, together with a scattering of little-organized liberal elements and the larger part of the labor movement. At the center of this unwieldy coalition sat the compromising and conciliating figure of F.D.R., whose political capital in the faction-ridden party had always been his ability to harmonize its conflicting elements.

It is now clear how deep these tensions cut into Roosevelt's own official family, how involved that family was with strong currents of private ambition in the struggle to inherit his leadership. Southerners like Hull and Garner resented Roosevelt's dalliance with the Left, and often felt that they were being personally bypassed. Machine Democrats from the North, whose simple devotion to party is raised to a major virtue in Farley's book, widely shared Farley's annoyance at the risks which they felt Roosevelt took of disrupting the national organization.

What Roosevelt failed to do—and no man could have done it within the framework of the Democratic Party—was to shape his alliance into an enduring agency of liberalism. It remained a temporary alliance, formed under the banner of a glamorous and persuasive leader who brought success to the party; it began to crack while the leader was still alive; it disintegrated within a few years of his death. Some of its members are now with Truman, some with Wallace, some with Thurmond, and some with Walter Reuther or any other man who will step forward to give the labor wing political leadership.*

Roosevelt came to power at a time when the greater part of the American public had been shocked out of its traditional ideology. The national faith, and national policy, had been based upon the enormous 19th Century expansion of the country, and its legacy of individualism, faith in opportunity, and optimism about future growth. Within the framework of that belief the role of the Federal Government was kept to a minimum: it was to regulate abuses of the competitive system, check monopoly, heal occasional sore spots in the economy, like those left by the railroads, and otherwise let things alone.

Hoover had been as resolutely loyal to that credo as conditions would allow, and he had failed. Roosevelt intuitively understood that he must be bolder and more experimental, but he had only a vague and unsteady conception of what should be done. He went on anyway, boldly, and with a deft political sense, but without an economic philosophy or a capacity for skillful administration. A tremendous amount of social evolution was telescoped into the six years after 1932—reforms of the sort that had been developing in England since the 1880's.

At such an accelerated pace mistakes

* Henry A. Wallace was the Progressive party candidate for President in 1948; J. Strom Thurmond was the states' rights candidate in that year.—Ed.

would have been inevitable under the most apt economic and administrative leadership, and Roosevelt was not apt. (Henry L. Stimson calls him the poorest administrator with whom he was ever associated.) The New Deal was a patchwork of inconsistencies, reflecting the various social pressures that made it and the absence of firm central guidance. As in the case of the Social Security Act, many excellent principles were embodied in ill-conceived laws.

Despite his superficiality, his tendency to *play* at politics, his failure to contemplate his means, there is a redeeming undercurrent of humanity in Roosevelt that few of his critics have failed to acknowledge. I suspect that he was happiest when he was steering the course of American development "a little to the left of center," in his memorable phrase. There, at any rate, his appeal to radicals and progressives lies. He was much concerned with his historical reputation, and seems to have felt that it was his standing as a man of good will that would sustain him. In one of his more mellow speeches he once reminded his listeners of Dante's saying that justice will weigh in different scales the sins of the warm-hearted and the sins of the cold-blooded. . . .

The point at which F.D.R. seems most vulnerable as a man, however, is in his easy-going view of the responsibilities of power. Lord Acton's maxim says that power corrupts. Roosevelt had the sort of personality that lends itself to corruption in Lord Acton's sense. I do not mean, of course, that he aspired to become a dictator, as his enemies used to say, or that he aimed at a sadistic or self-aggrandizing use of his position. But it does seem that his grasp of his responsibilities was neither intellectually nor

spiritually profound. Here he suffers by comparison with men of the spiritual gravity of Lincoln and Wilson.

I have in mind an incident at the Teheran conference reported by Elliott Roosevelt. Stalin proposed a toast to the coming summary execution of the German war criminals—50,000 of them, as he hoped the figure would be—and Churchill angrily challenged him by insisting that there be proper legal trials for everyone. F.D.R. stepped in with the "witticism," as Elliott calls it, that the number ought to be pared down to perhaps 49,500. Roosevelt, to be sure, was only trying to smooth over a conflict between his allies. And he was only jesting. That is clear enough: but what is pertinent here is that *that* was the way he tried to smooth over conflicts, and that *that* was the way he jested.

Since every generation revises history, it would be naive to hope that we can easily arrive at some final estimate of F.D.R. Probably his wartime and worldwide leadership, as in the case of Woodrow Wilson, will be the primary basis upon which he will be judged. And that part of his career is highly vulnerable.

There seems to be a law governing the conduct of diplomatic affairs similar to Gresham's law of monetary circulation which tells us that bad money drives out good. At best, the conduct of diplomacy has never been open, candid, and democratic. But when there is a dictator or bloc of dictators with aggressive aims, this Gresham's law of diplomacy begins to operate. The statemen of more democratic powers, menaced by a dictator who can move swiftly and decisively without fear of interference at home, must either plan their counter-strategy in a deceitful or high-handed manner or take the risk that democratic restraints will impair their policies.

So far as it was possible, F.D.R. chose the former course. During the early months of World War II he concluded that a victory of the Axis powers would be a great menace to the peace and security of the United States. Public opinion concurred with this conclusion, but there remained a difference of opinion as to how far the nation should go. In time the Administration became convinced that outright participation was necessary. Secretary Stimson favored a candid statement of the situation to the public; Roosevelt preferred a more circuitous course.

The distinguished diplomatic historian, Prof. Thomas A. Bailey, analyzing this dilemma in his book, *The Man in the Street,* argues that candor would have been "foolhardy," and that Roosevelt would have been defeated in the election of 1940.

"Roosevelt repeatedly deceived the American people during the period before Pearl Harbor," says Prof. Bailey, but deceived them into acting in accordance with their best interests, and posterity may "thank him for it."

It is a nice question in political ethics. Posterity may also wonder whether the long-range conduct of affairs in accordance with such principles of benevolent deceit is consistent with democracy. As Prof. Bailey remarks in the same book, "In a dictatorship the masses must be deceived; in a democracy they must be educated."

Now it seems entirely possible that we may arrive in a few years at an entirely different perspective on what was accomplished in the war. During the war most people were persuaded that the United States was fighting, if for nothing more, to prevent the emergence in Europe and Asia of a totalitarian bloc of continental proportions which would remain a standing menace to its security and force its people to maintain a permanent garrison state. There is a growing feeling that, after all the sacrifices of the war, we have arrived at that position today; the power we are opposing is hardly more pacific or civilized than the Axis, although somewhat less formidable.

Prof. Nathaniel Peffer, writing on "Democracy Losing by Default" in the current *Political Science Quarterly,* observes: "We of the victors have escaped subjugation and enjoyed the emotional satisfaction of exacting retribution from the Germans and Japanese, but in all else we have lost. We and the world are worse off for our victory. We have not even the assurance of a transient peace, to say nothing of a long truce.... On all the evidence before us, judged by historical precedents, we are now in the state prelude to war, analogous to the years 1912 and 1937."

It may be true, of course, that we and the rest of the world would have been in a much worse position if another course had been adopted. And yet if other thoughtful people are beginning to ponder as earnestly as Prof. Peffer the balance between sacrifices and gains, Roosevelt's reputation will have to share in the revaluation.

Certainly, in the light of the immense tragedy of our time, his gay and light-hearted assumption of power, his easy confidence in his expedients, and his pathetic conviction that he could arrive at some sort of workable and durable understanding with the Soviet power by impressing such a man as Stalin with his goodwill and charms, are hardly imposing qualities. ....

BASIL RAUCH (1908–   ), professor of history at
Barnard College, wrote the first substantial history
of the New Deal. His work was a careful, detailed
analysis imbued with the conviction that what is being
described is a portentous and admirable development
in American life. He is typical of a generation of
historians whose personal commitment to the values
of the New Deal has been strong and unshakable.*

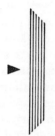

The First New Deal

The President had decided to hold
Congress in special session beyond the
immediate banking emergency, in order
to put through a group of basic recovery
measures while the atmosphere of emergency helped to minimize opposition.
Unemployment and farm relief were
announced as his objectives. Before the
legislative mills had ceased to grind at
the end of the famous "hundred days"
a large number of important laws had
been passed.

On March 16 [1933] a draft of the
Agricultural Adjustment Bill was sent
to Congress with a message urging its
passage in time to restrict the spring
planting of crops in accordance with its
provisions. The Bill was the product of
the President's campaign pledge, and of

general agreement among farm and administration leaders to experiment with
the Voluntary Domestic Allotment Plan,
but its provisions were so broad that
either one, or both, of two methods
might be used. The more conservative and nationalistic scheme, sometimes
called the Clair Plan, found its chief
advocate in George N. Peek. He had
been associated with General Hugh S.
Johnson in the Moline Plow Company
of Illinois, where both had learned the
lesson that farmers who were not prosperous could not make industry prosperous by buying its products. Much
thought and search for the solution of
the problem had finally brought them to
Washington in early spring of 1933 with
plans which were incorporated into the

* From Basil Rauch, *The History of the New Deal* (New York: [Creative Age Press],
Farrar, Straus and Cudahy, Inc., 1944).

First New Deal, Johnson's in the program for industrial, and Peek's in the program for agricultural recovery. The plan which Peek advocated aimed to give the farmers the benefit of tariff protection which their surpluses ordinarily denied them because they had to be sold in foreign markets whose low prices therefore determined prices in the American market. The plan was to allot money received by the government from agricultural import taxes to every farmer in an amount proportionate to the percentage of his crop which would be sold in the domestic market. No curtailment or regulation of the farmer's production would be required except in years and areas of superabundant yield, when farmers would be called upon to destroy a portion of the growing crop in order to qualify for their money allotments. High tariffs would be maintained, and ordinary surpluses would be marketed abroad with the same aggressive help of the government which had supported the export of manufactures during the Republican administrations. Peek claimed that this scheme would minimize bureaucratic control of the farmer while giving him those benefits of economic nationalist policy which industry already enjoyed.

With the substitution of an excise tax on processors of farm products as the source of money benefits to be paid to farmers, Peek's scheme was incorporated in the Rainey Bill and passed the Senate in 1932. Then it was quietly shelved in the House. He and leaders of the main farm organizations thereupon supported the candidacy of Roosevelt because they had been led to believe that their plan would be adopted by him. According to Peek's account, after the election professors and lawyers led by Rexford G.

Tugwell and Jerome Frank, and the "mystical idealist," Henry Wallace, took control of farm legislation for the new administration and wrote a bill which embodied the alternative scheme for carrying out the Domestic Allotment Plan. This scheme was for acreage control by the government and would abolish the farm surplus, even in normal years and before the crop was planted, by paying rentals to farmers on acreage taken out of production. Coöperation by farmers was voluntary, but few were likely to refuse to receive checks for not cultivating a percentage of their acres, and Peek believed the scheme to be "collectivist" because it entailed "regulation" of the farmers, as well as "internationalist" because it would benefit the whole world by removing the American surpluses from the international market and thereby raise the world price of farm commodities. It was linked to low tariff and other internationalist ideals and, Peek was convinced, would not work. . . .

The Domestic Allotment Plan was supported chiefly by larger farmers who produced the staple subject to export, such as wheat and cotton, which would be included in the Plan. These farmers constituted the strength of the Farm Bureau Federation, the National Grange, and several other organizations which wielded great influence on the Congressmen of the bi-partisan Farm Bloc. Peek's statement that these farm organizations had little to do with the Agricultural Adjustment Bill must be taken in the narrow sense of actual participation in its writing, because limitation of farm production by a scheme such as the Domestic Allotment Plan had long been their chief demand, especially since the failure of Hoover's Marketing Act. On the other hand, the National Farmers Union and the Farmers National Holiday Association represented the smaller farmers and tenants who were less dependent on staple crops and therefore less interested in the Domestic Allotment Plan. . . .

When it was finally passed as an administration measure and signed on May 12, the Agricultural Adjustment Act was an omnibus which gave the farmers of the country their three main demands of the preceding half-century and longer: protection against the ruinous effect on prices of their surplus crops, inflated currency with which to pay their debts, and cheap credit. No law had promised the farmer so much since the Homestead Act of 1863. If the law did not introduce Utopia, it was not for lack of willingness by the administration to heed the farmer's voice in the spring of 1933.

Unemployment relief was the second immediate objective of the administration. On March 21, the President sent a message to Congress asking for three types of legislation, none of which departed far in principle from the relief policies of the Hoover administration. Two of the requests were quickly met by establishment of the Civilian Conservation Corps which provided 250,000 unemployed young men with little more than subsistence wages as workers in the national forests, and the Federal Emergency Relief Administration which made grants to the states for direct relief. The CCC was a type of public works activity which the Hoover administration had not developed, while the FERA grants were gifts as contrasted with the loans to the states for direct relief which Hoover had inaugurated in June, 1932. The third request was met in Title II of the National Industrial Recovery Act passed in June. This Title established the Public Works Administration and was a simple

expansion of the Hoover policy of providing employment by the construction of public buildings, roads, and other traditional federal works. The appropriations for the CCC, FERA, and PWA exceeded the outlays for relief by the preceding administration, but they did not approximate the great expenditures which began in 1935, when, for the period of the Second New Deal, a fundamentally new relief policy was inaugurated to provide federal employment at security wage scales to all employables. Meanwhile a relief policy acceptable to conservatives was intended to mitigate the worst suffering without solving the unemployment problem. . . .

The National Industrial Recovery Bill . . . was based on the assumption that labor and industry would share the benefits of recovery, and to this end both interests were granted government support in the achievement of their programs. In the famous Section 7A, labor was promised the inclusion in industrial codes of unspecified minimum-wages and maximum-hours rules, and was guaranteed the right of collective bargaining with employers through representatives freely chosen by employees. For businessmen, limitation of production and exemption of codes from the antitrust laws were provided. The question of the degree of governmental control in the drawing up of codes was left to a tug-of-war between the trade associations which were given the right to formulate them, and the government which could reject them and promulgate codes on its own motion. Violators of code agreements could be prosecuted before the federal courts and punished. The President was left free to establish whatever administrative agencies he deemed necessary. The Bill was considered by the

President to be a deliberate step away from the philosophy of "equalitarianism and *laissez faire*" which Hoover's failure and his own election had proven to be "bankrupt." Ideally, the system envisaged would consist of separate institutions of self-government for both labor and industry, with the government requiring them to coöperate and preventing either one from injuring the other or the public....

The National Industrial Recovery Act was passed by large majorities and signed on June 16. The President said that history would probably record it as "the most important and far-reaching legislation ever enacted by the American Congress.... Its goal is the assurance of a reasonable profit to industry and living wages for labor." Thus were added to the farmers the second and third main interest groups to whom the administration during the First New Deal tried strenuously to grant their main demands.

The chief purpose of the AAA and NIRA was recovery. They dominated the First New Deal, and the administration's first crusades were organized around them. Three other laws were passed during the Hundred Days the chief purpose of which was reform rather than recovery. These attracted less attention at the time, but their greater permanency and their capacity for organic growth make them significant. Each of the three laws had been promised in the Democratic platform, and was a specific application of the reform traditions which had been interrupted when Woodrow Wilson left the White House.

The Tennessee Valley Authority Act of May 18 was a victory for those who, without discussing socialist theory, insisted that the government own and operate for the benefit of the people hydro-electric plants on the great waterways of the nation in order to prevent private corporations from exploiting these vast resources for private profit. Republican administrations had nowhere shown themselves more ineffective than in their inability to find any solution other than shutting down the government's great wartime power and munitions plant at Muscle Shoals. Senator George W. Norris of Nebraska had conducted a relentless struggle to end the waste of power on the Tennessee River and to place it at the service of the people of the region. The TVA was a personal victory for him as well as for the public policy which Roosevelt had painstakingly developed while Governor of New York....

The Securities Act of May 27 originated in the conviction of liberals over many years that a federal "blue-sky" law was needed to protect the public from fraud and misrepresentation in the issuance, manipulation, and sale of stocks and other securities. The depression had thrown glaring light on the unscrupulous purposes behind many securities issues, the devious methods by which insiders rigged the stock market, and the deceptions practiced by high-pressure salesmen who gulled the small investor. Correction of these abuses was a part of the Democratic platform. Confusion of counsel separated regulation of securities issues and sales from the allied problem of stock-exchange regulation, postponed action on the latter until 1934, and resulted in a bill drawn chiefly by Felix Frankfurter and hastily passed without hearings by Congress. Its main provisions were that new issues of securities be registered with the Federal Trade Commission along with a statement of the financial position of the company, and that the same information be given to all purchasers of the issue. "Let the seller beware!" was substituted for the older slogan: misrepresentation was made subject to prosecution. Whether or not this Truth-in-Securities Act was cumbersome, as its revision in 1934 argues, and hindered the flotation of new issues in 1933, it was of less pressing importance than the regulation of stock exchanges. In the absence of the latter reform, a speculative Wall Street boom, garnished by all the abuses of the pre-depression era, threatened to discount recovery before the administration's program could be put into effect and purchasing power be increased to keep pace with rising prices.

The Glass-Steagall Banking Act of June 16 established three reforms which most bankers as well as liberals had come to believe were necessary to prevent repetition of the abuses which had aggravated the boom, the depression, and the banking crisis. Investment banking was separated from commercial banking so that affiliates could no longer be used by bankers for speculation with their depositors' money. The Federal Deposit Insurance Corporation was established to afford a government guaranty of bank deposits under $5,000, and thus remove the motive for runs on banks by small depositors such as had occurred prior to March 4. The Federal Reserve Board was given powers over interest rates and other factors which would enable it to prevent excessive speculation with borrowed money.

The TVA, the Securities Act, and the Banking Act were all sustained by the Supreme Court, while the chief recovery laws, AAA and NIRA, were invalidated. This remarkable fact, usually forgotten at the time of the struggle over the President's court reorganization plan, made the reform legislation of the First New Deal more important for the future than the recovery legislation which was at the time the administration's chief concern. . . .

[The NRA and AAA did not bring the immediate benefits that labor, industry, and agriculture expected.]

The most important action taken by the administration in the fall of 1933 to save the recovery program was in the field of gold policy. The drop in the international exchange value of the dollar when it was divorced from gold in the spring had been accompanied by a sharp rise in domestic prices, stimulation of exports, and restraint of imports. On July 8 it was decided that, in the President's words: "Since the Administration's efforts to raise commodity prices were meeting with success, and other American exporters were finding that their world markets were expanding . . . American gold-mining interests could obtain the benefits of world gold prices" by the government relaxing the restrictions on gold exports. But this action was perhaps premature and influenced the end of the domestic boom later in the month. When it became apparent by the middle of October that NRA and AAA were failing to develop recovery of industrial production, employment and payrolls, and farm prices, it was announced on October 22 that an experiment based on the "commodity-dollar" theory of Professor Warren would be undertaken.

The dollar had ceased its rapid decline in August. The Warren plan called for artificial measures to force the gold value of the dollar to decline still farther, and its sponsors predicted that commodity prices would rise proportionately. Since the prices of manufactured goods were recovering successfully, the administration's first interest was in stimulating farm prices, and it was hoped that these, being more dependent on world prices than the former, would be the greater beneficiaries of the Warren scheme to raise American prices higher than the world level. Furthermore, farm exports were chiefly dependent on price conditions, while exports of manufactures depended more on quality and on patent cartels, so that farm exports could be expected to benefit specially by forced dollar devaluation. . . .

The second front on which the President attacked the threatened collapse was unemployment relief. The NRA campaign to expand employment and production was failing. The President had been doubtful from the beginning that the PWA would put an appreciable number of the unemployed to work, because of the restriction on it that only the conventional types of public construction and repair projects might be undertaken. Besides this, Secretary Ickes as its Administrator had proceeded in fear of waste and graft with so much caution that very few new projects were opened by fall. Relief rolls began to rise again with the business reaction in October. The prospect of another winter of increasing unemployment determined the President to act.

Harry Hopkins was the most important figure in helping to evolve the administration's relief policy. He had been a social worker in Christadora House, New York City, before his appointment by Governor Roosevelt as chairman of the New York State Temporary Relief Administration. Early in 1933 he became head of the FERA, and after the experience with it and the other extension of Hoover relief policies, PWA, he helped to plan new departures. The most important elements in Hopkins' conception of relief were that the federal government should provide work relief for employables rather than merely funds for direct relief to be administered by the states, that minimum wage rates higher than relief payments should be paid for labor and that the skills of the unemployed should be used and developed. The social effect of giving work at all levels of skill instead of a dole to the unemployed would be profound, and the labor market would be influenced in ways immediately favorable to labor rather than employers by fair wage standards on federal work projects. The centralization of relief administration and the use of federal credit resources would make possible the substitution of nation-wide campaigns to "prime the pump" of recovery by injecting purchasing power into the lowest level of the economic structure, for uncoördinated and financially weak local-relief activities.

A first step towards realization of these objectives was taken on November 8, when the President announced the creation of the Civil Works Administration to put four million unemployed persons to work immediately on federal "made-work" projects. Funds were allocated from FERA and PWA appropriations supplemented by local governments. Wages were paid which represented a great increase in the purchasing power of the unemployed as compared with relief payments. The administrative machinery was entirely federal, with Hopkins at its head.

Confined on one side to work which could be undertaken more quickly and with less expenditure for materials than PWA projects, and on the other by scrupulous avoidance of competition with private enterprise, the CWA made-work projects were frequently no more useful than raking leaves. But the CWA achieved its main purposes. By January over four million persons were at work, suffering which would have been intensified with a fourth winter of increasing unemployment was minimized, and the sudden injection of almost a billion dollars into the hands of buyers helped to sustain the nation's economy. The program was not intended to be permanent, but a solution of immediate problems, and it was ended by April 1. The experiment served as an intermediate stage in the evolution of relief policy from the initial adoption of Hoover policies which appealed chiefly to business interests, to the full-fledged instrumentation in the Works Progress Administration of 1935 of the Hopkins conception, which appealed chiefly to labor interests and became the relief policy of the Second New Deal.

The third action taken to support recovery was the adjustment of NRA regulations to improve the position of small business and labor. On October 22 businessmen in small towns were exempted from observing the Blanket Code, price increases by manufacturers were made subject to investigation, and machinery for handling complaints against business practices was established. On December 16 the National Labor Board's powers were increased as a result of "several flagrant cases of defiance of the Board by large employers of labor." The Board had been established to preserve industrial peace by "passing" on disputes arising under Section 7A. Now its powers were defined to include mediation, conciliation, and arbitration. These alterations of NRA, slight in themselves, nevertheless were the first official recognition of what statistical definitions of the

results of the experiment made clear: that NRA was not providing equal benefits for all groups; rather big business was turning it to its own purposes at the expense of small business, labor, and consumers. . . .

The year 1934 was one of transition from the First to the Second New Deal. The CWA which was in full swing at the beginning of the year represented a transitional experiment in relief policy. The stabilization of the dollar in January and the Reciprocity Trade Agreements Act of June ended economic nationalism in foreign policy, if the Silver Purchase Act of June be excepted. Acreage control of farm production was fully established. Bitter controversies over NRA featured the slow shift of policy in the field of relations among government, industry, and labor. The year ended with striking approval at the polls of the administration's course, and with momentous decisions which launched major policies of the Second New Deal in 1935. . . .

The first full year of AAA operation and the tragedy of the Dust Bowl increased rather than diminished the proportions of the farm problem. Administration experiments were made with resettlement and subsistence farming projects, but they remained minute in scope, and little more was heard of "the over-balance of population in our industrial centers," or of "engaging on a national scale in a redistribution," as proposed in the President's Inaugural Address. The speeding up of the mechanization and concentration of agriculture in larger units and the displacement of tenants and sharecroppers, which the AAA was furthering, was intensified by the drought and dust storms, and worked to swell the ranks of a new class of migrant farm laborers, whose poverty and helplessness were unmatched by any other group of the population. Their lack of a fixed residence made them practically ineligible for relief and uninteresting to politicians. States, counties, and towns raised "immigration" barriers against them. Their labor, and their children's, was excessively exploited by large farms, which were not subject to NRA codes. Their lack of experience and of fixed employment with a stationary group made the tactics of industrial labor unionism virtually useless to them. The AAA broadly satisfied the large farmers who produced staples which were included in the program. The administration's farm credit system reached farmers whose land produced some sort of income. But the problems of farmers who were dusted out or otherwise lost their land, of tenants, sharecroppers, and migrants were multiplying, and the administration did not for several more years formulate a program which would reach these most depressed groups and constitute a Second New Deal in agriculture.

The chief controversy and the one most fruitful of change in administration policy during the transition from the First to the Second New Deal concerned NRA. Opposition to the experiment mounted steadily. The administration never denied that the rise in industrial prices and profits was outrunning the rise in employment and purchasing power.

The charge that NRA fostered monopoly was vigorously denied by the administration from time to time, but on several occasions in 1934 it also took action designed to break down monopolistic tendencies. Thus on January 20 the President issued an Executive Order:

to provide a practical and rapid way for mak-

ing effective those provisions of the National Industrial Recovery Act that were designed to prevent persons, under the guise of purported sanctions contained in codes ... from engaging in monopolistic practices or practices tending to eliminate, oppress or discriminate against small enterprises.

Complaints against monopoly were empowered to appeal their cases from the code authorities to the Federal Trade Commission or the Department of Justice....

Rightly or wrongly, opponents of NRA believed that General [Hugh] Johnson* had not carried out the intention of the National Industrial Recovery Act, but had unbalanced the codes and their administration in favor of big business. Johnson now took the view that with code-making virtually at an end, and compliance and enforcement emerging as the main problems, he should resign and his functions be subdivided among the members of a board. With this the President agreed. Rumors that Secretary [Francis] Perkins† and Donald Richberg were instrumental in securing his resignation because they found the General too favorable to big business and too high-handed in his methods were, in Johnson's account, not entirely unfounded.

In August, General Johnson returned from a tour of the country and, possibly as a result of his contact with public opinion, exempted many more categories of small business from all code provisions except those guaranteeing collective bargaining and forbidding child labor. On September 24 he resigned from the office of Administrator of NRA. Three days later the President ordered his former office abolished and a Na-

* Chief administrator of the NRA—Ed.
† Secretary of labor—Ed.

tional Industrial Recovery Board composed of five officials to take its place. . . . On October 22 the new Board announced that code provisions to limit production would no longer be enforced.

If under NRA the administration had permitted big business to consolidate monopoly with government sanction, and had encouraged substitution of employer-dominated company unions for independent labor unions, the charge of fascism might have acquired some validity. As it was, the monopolistic features of NRA were being whittled away by the end of 1934. The chief reason was the refusal of business to enter into the coöperative spirit on which the experiment was predicated, to share the benefits of recovery with other groups, or to observe in good faith the provisions of Section 7A in return for its own privileges. Business had won official recognition for its own trade associations and their program, but it had refused to grant similar recognition to independent labor unions and their program. It had enjoyed a virtually free hand in writing and administering the codes, but it had exercised its power chiefly with regard to the immediate advantages which could be won for itself. It did not accept the analysis that the depression had been caused by a failure of purchasing power and that recovery could only be founded on its expansion. The bitterness with which businessmen were beginning to oppose the administration was perhaps partly a recognition that their collectivity had thrown away a chance to remain high in administration councils by failing to pursue a statesmanlike policy during the early days of NRA, and had failed to retrieve its mistake when it had a second chance in the spring of 1934. . . .

The administration intended that col-lective bargaining be freely entered into by employers and employees, and it frequently urged that labor refrain from striking while employers were given an opportunity to comply. But the common refusal of employers to meet with representatives of independent unions under any circumstances; their haste to organize company unions which were amenable to their own influence; the host of knotty questions of interpretation of Section 7A which employers precipitated; and the reluctance of the administration to resort to sanctions to enforce labor rights increased the impatience of labor and helped produce another and greater wave of strikes. The number of strikes and of workers involved in the spring and summer of 1934 exceeded all figures since 1922. The militia forces of 19 states were called out, and with police, deputy sheriffs, and company guards killed 46 workers. In 1932, union recognition was the issue in less than 20 per cent of the strikes called, but in 1934 recognition of a union as bargaining agent under Section 7A was the issue in almost 50 per cent of the strikes. . . .

Senator Robert F. Wagner of New York, after serving as Chairman of the National Labor Board during its first half-year, concluded that the purposes of Section 7A could be secured only if new legislation were enacted which, as he stated to Congress, would protect the principle of collective bargaining from employer-dominated unions and prevent the latter from destroying or supplanting free labor unions. On March 1, he introduced in the Senate the Labor Disputes Bill to prohibit "unfair labor practices" by employers, among which the following were enumerated: the initiation and financing of company unions, interference with employees' free choice of their representatives, and refusal to recognize or bargain with employee representatives. It also called for the creation of a permanent labor board with power to impose penalties in order to enforce the provisions of the law, mediate disputes, and conduct elections to determine employees' representatives. . . .

The conservative press, employers' trade associations, and businessmen in general bitterly opposed the Wagner Labor Disputes Bill. The *New York Herald Tribune* called it the road to fascism. The contrary argument, that independent labor unions were destroyed under fascism, and exactly such employer-dominated organizations as the American company unions substituted by force, was advanced by liberals. The Senate hearing revealed that businessmen heartily approved the NRA as it was then functioning. President Emery of the National Association of Manufacturers defended company unions because they were "modern," and admitted, when pressed by Senator Wagner, that he had opposed Section 7A from the beginning and supported only the parts of the Recovery Act which gave business special privileges. Emery complained that a labor board composed of representatives of both employers and employees could not be impartial because basic interests of the two groups were conflicting. On the other hand, General Counsel Edmonds of the Philadelphia Chamber of Commerce objected to the Bill precisely because it impressed him as having been written by "a man who had been reading Marx on Class War, and thought all employers and employees were standing in opposite corners making faces at each other." President Harriman of the United States Chamber of Commerce feared that the Bill would undo the good

which had come from the Recovery Act, and proposed reliance upon General Johnson to work out labor problems with the existing machinery. Johnson failed to appear before the Commitee, and it was understood that he disapproved any ban on company unions. . . .

The attitude of the administration towards the Labor Disputes Bill was expected to be decisive. It squarely presented to the President the issue whether collective bargaining under NRA should be conducted by company unions or by independent unions. That the President was willing to give businessmen further opportunity to prove their contention that the aims of Section 7A and of the recovery program could be achieved through company unions was indicated during his intervention late in March in the threatened automobile strike. After conferences with leaders of both sides, he arranged a settlement under which the new Automobile Labor Board could recognize company unions as bargaining agents: "The Government makes it clear that it favors no particular union or particular form of employee organization or representation." No restrictions were placed upon employer financing and controlling company unions in the automobile industry. The general opinion of the Senate was that the President had by this agreement registered his disapproval of the Wagner Labor Disputes Bill.

Senator Wagner accordingly permitted his Bill to be amended to remove most of the restrictions on domination by employers of company unions. President Harriman of the Chamber of Commerce thereupon said that the Bill was unnecessary because the President had already sanctioned company unions. Senator Wagner then revised his Bill and secured

White House approval of restoration of some restrictions on company unions. The bill was up for final vote on the same day that the President reached an agreement to settle the strike of steel workers which was to begin that day. This settlement, like that of the automobile strike, made possible the use by employers of company unions. Senator Robinson prevented the Wagner Bill from coming to a vote and secured the substitution of a resolution which merely gave statutory authority to the Executive Orders of February which had provided for elections and prosecutions. Senator Robinson, as Democratic floor leader, was acting on the President's request. Senator Wagner deferred to the President, saying that he was ready to accept the latter's judgment that further trial should be permitted before employer-dominated unions were rejected as bargaining agents. Other progressive Senators were reluctant to support the resolution. Senator Cutting of New Mexico protested that "the new deal is being strangled in the house of its friends." Nevertheless the resolution was pushed through both houses.

On June 29, the President abolished the old National Labor Board and established the new National Labor Relations Board, which permitted the appointment of new members and the resignation of Senator Wagner, whose Bill had no doubt made employers dissatisfied with him.

Thus the administration went very far to avoid coercion of employers and to encourage voluntary compliance with Section 7A. The fall in production, employment, and payrolls in May did not lead the administration to change its labor policy, nor did the new outbreak of strikes which reached epidemic pro-

portions in September. Through the summer months, the President in his public speeches stressed the need for the unity and coöperation of all groups in working for recovery. His mood was not friendly towards the partisans of labor, rather he sought to conciliate businessmen. Possibly he believed that the relaxation of the controls on production and prices in the NRA codes, coupled with a free hand granted to business in the matter of company unions would induce an industrial revival. At any rate, on September 30, when he announced the reorganization of NRA he offered business "a specific trial period of industrial peace" during which they might use their company unions to carry out rather than circumvent the collective bargaining clause of Section 7A. A month later the President in an address to the American Bankers' Association renewed his plea for the coöperation of business on equal terms with other groups:

The time is ripe for an alliance of all forces intent upon the business of recovery. In such an alliance will be found business and banking, agriculture and industry, and labor and capital. What an all-America team that would be! The possibilities of such a team kindle the imagination.

Attempts to conciliate business did not prevent the organization in August of the Liberty League, a combination of conservative Democrats and industrial leaders, including Jouett Shouse, Al Smith, and members of the DuPont family, to fight the "radicalism" of the New Deal. The Liberty League was intended to make the rights of property supreme over all other rights, to stiffen the resistance of businessmen to the President's program to discourage concessions to labor, and to secure the election of an anti-New Deal Congress in the November elections. In the last purpose at least it was unsuccessful. And its extreme attacks on the administration did not strengthen advocates of conciliation on either side.

In spite of his seeming support of company unions, the President retained the confidence of labor. Dissatisfaction with this aspect of the administration program was outweighed by the recognition that other policies worked in labor's favor. A far-reaching program of social security had been initiated. The Railway Retirement Act of June 27 provided pensions for railroad workers after thirty years' service or at an age of sixty-five, the cost to be borne one-third by themselves and two-thirds by the companies. And on June 29, the President had appointed the Commitee on Economic Security to prepare plans for a universal program of unemployment and old-age pension insurance, and health and child welfare benefits. New ground was being broken to meet one of the fundamental needs of labor and bring American social legislation abreast of common practice in other industrial nations.

Government regulation of business enterprise was extended to several new fields during 1934. The Securities Exchange Act of June 6 established the Securities and Exchange Commission and charged it with the enforcement of the Securities Act of 1933 and with the prevention of excessive speculation, marginal trading, and manipulation of prices by stock-exchange operators. The Communications Act of June 19 created the Federal Communications Commission to exercise controls over telegraph, cable, and radio corporations similar to those of the Interstate Commerce Commission over transportation. After revelations of fraud in the letting of air mail contracts

which occurred under the Hoover administration, and a disastrous attempt to fly the mails by the Army, the Air Mail Act of June 12 was passed to return mail flying to private companies under rigid controls calculated to prevent further fraud. Kidnaping and other crimes were made subject to federal law. These laws were additions to the permanent body of progressive reforms and had long been demanded by liberals. But General Smedley D. Butler created a sensation when he told a House Committee that during the summer of 1934 a group of Wall Street brokers had urged him to lead a fascist march on Washington and overthrow the government in order to protect business interests.

When the President approached the first test of his administration in the November Congressional elections, he had largely lost the support which business had given him during the banking crisis and the first NRA campaign. The concessions which had been made in regard to company unions did not offset the opposition which the many far-reaching reforms produced among businessmen. Nor did the opposition of organized labor to company unions, bitter as it was, prevent the administration from holding the support of labor, which again joined with farmers to elect still larger Democratic majorities to Congress. The President and his aggressive attack on the depression, besides reforms which satisfied the public demand for correction of business abuses which the depression years had revealed, captured the public imagination and won a degree of loyalty among his supporters which no President since Wilson had enjoyed.

The Republican Party had no constructive program to offer as an alternative to the New Deal, and appealed only to fears that "limitless inflation," "domination of an all-powerful central government," and other perils were in the offing. Republican strength fell in the Senate from 35 to 25 and in the House from 113 to 103, and Republican progressives or partial supporters of the administration fared better than those who campaigned on the Party platform.

These results, which violated the usual rule that an administration loses Congressional support in mid-term elections, were described by Charles A. Beard as "thunder on the left." The new Congress was expected to demand an end of concessions to business and a wholehearted farmer-labor program for recovery and reform. Although the National Association of Manufacturers remained intransigent after the election, the prospect of a more "radical" Congress caused the leaders of the Chamber of Commerce to believe that possibly a mistake was being made in not accepting the President's offers to business of coöperation. Now they made an effort to rally to his support. A series of conferences was held between business leaders and the President. The former made known their support of the more conservative administration leaders, such as Secretaries Hull, Morgenthau, and Roper, Jesse Jones and Professor Moley, and their opposition to the "radicals," including Secretaries Ickes and Perkins, and Hopkins and Tugwell.

Whatever confidences were exchanged and understandings were reached in these conferences, the unbalanced character of recovery could not be gainsaid. In his Message to the new Congress the President found it impossible to say that recovery, after a year and a half, was creating anything besides "substantial benefits to our agricultural population, increased industrial activity, and profits to our merchants." Congress was thereupon asked to legislate a new program which should add labor to the beneficiaries of recovery, and the main program of the Second New Deal, after a long season of reluctance, was launched.

EDGAR E. ROBINSON, (1887–   ), Margaret Byrne
Professor of American History at Stanford University,
speaks for a different generation, both in age and in
outlook, than does Rauch. Robinson has long been
close to Herbert Hoover, and is presently writing a
biography of the former President. Not surprisingly,
the underlying viewpoint of his study of Roosevelt's
leadership is that the New Deal posed a substantial
and dangerous challenge to traditional values in
American life.*

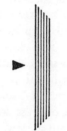

An Unaccustomed Road

... The financial crisis was real; no one could doubt it. The financial life of the nation was in a state of inanimate suspension. In the view of the outgoing administration, this condition was the result of the unwillingness of the incoming administration to co-operate in measures to restore confidence. The mass of the people were in a mood of despair. The millions of unemployed had yet to see any system of relief at the hands of the national government. For the able-bodied and the healthy there were no precedents for government aid.

President Roosevelt believed that the first of his problems was the restoration of confidence. His own words at the time embody his view of the necessity facing him.

Values have shrunken to fantastic levels; taxes have risen; our ability to pay has fallen; government of all kinds is faced by serious curtailment of income; the means of exchange are frozen in the currents of trade; the withered leaves of industrial enterprise lie on every side; farmers find no markets for their produce; the savings of many years in thousands of families are gone.... More important, a host of unemployed citizens face the grim problem of existence, and an equally great number toil with little return. Only a foolish optimist can deny the dark realities of the moment.

Yet a radio commentator had noted that on his way to the Capitol, Mr.

---

* From *The Roosevelt Leadership*, by Edgar E. Robinson. Copyright 1955 by J. B. Lippincott Company. Published by J. B. Lippincott Company.

Roosevelt looked "magnificently confident." According to his wife, the new President "believed in God and His guidance. He felt that human beings were given tasks to perform and with those tasks the ability and strength to put them through. He could pray for help and guidance and have faith in his own judgment as a result. The church services that he always insisted on holding on Inauguration Day ... and whenever a great crisis impended were the expression of his religious faith."

Mr. Roosevelt felt that the inaugural address contained all the elements in his program. It was the conviction of those who formulated this program that his addresses in the campaign had foreshadowed every important element in the New Deal. Viewed in perspective, no such pronounced result as emerged had in fact been envisaged.

As one of his closest advisers at the time saw it, "We stood in the city of Washington on March 4th like a handful of marauders in hostile territory ... the Republican party had close to a monopoly of skillful, experienced administrators. To make matters worse, the business managers, established lawyers, and engineers from whose ranks top-drawer governmental executives so often come were, by and large, so partisan in their opposition to Roosevelt that he could scarcely be expected to tap those sources to the customary degree."

During the early phases of the first administration, conspicuous as personal advisers were Raymond Moley, Rexford G. Tugwell, Adolph Berle, Hugh Johnson, and of course Louis Howe and Henry Morgenthau, Jr. The work of each of these men in contributing to the determination of public policy deserves extensive examination. As the adminis-

tration moved into its second year, the influence of Secretary Ickes became very important. The contribution of such close associates as Henry Wallace, James Farley, William Woodin and Frances Perkins had become well known. Harry Hopkins was in a different category than any other adviser, as events were to show. Not coming to Washington until May 22, he became almost at once—in the eyes of eager commentators—the embodiment of the New Deal as it related to relief.

It was not clearly apparent at the time, even though much public attention was fixed upon these men, how important they were in the emerging pattern of government in the "progressive" spirit. The people as a whole had voted to take over their own government. That was Mr. Roosevelt's view. But they had to have men in government to do this work. Experts, not elected to office, were to aid the President in his task.

To identify Franklin Roosevelt with the attitude of these experts who seemed, during the years 1933-1937, to speak for the nation, is to misunderstand him completely. It is possible that the time may come when a product of professional training in the social sciences will be elected to the Presidency. By inclination or experience, Mr. Roosevelt was not of such a group, however much he valued and used their services and however often, on occasion, he used their language. When he spoke of the American people he meant, as he visualized them, a people with somewhat the same attitude toward democracy, toward party, toward progress, toward reform, that he had. He conceived of reformers as men of action, rather than as men of thought. Roosevelt and the People were one.

Clearly, semi-dictatorial powers had been granted the President. The Fascist press in Italy, commenting on the inaugural address, commended the cutting short of "the purposeless chatter of legislative assemblies.". . .

The President had explained his point of view at his first press conference on March 8 and "delighted" the press with his candor. On Sunday evening, March 12, Mr. Roosevelt outlined the banking situation to the nation in a fifteen-minute radio address. The commentator Will Rogers wrote, "Well, he made everybody understand it, even the bankers." When the "Beer Bill," amending the Volstead Act, passed the House 316-97, Rogers was saying, "I don't know what additional authority Roosevelt may ask, but give it to him, even if it's to drown all the boy babies. . . . It just shows you what a country can do when you take their affairs out of the hands of Congress."

The response of the country to the new leadership was immediate, and on the whole favorable. The vigorous support in definite Congressional action was proof that the President had successfully asserted aggressive leadership.

President Roosevelt saw the nation's emergency as long in the making. In amplifying his view of this in 1934, he wrote:

After the World War, a wholly unplanned pyramiding of production and of speculation had left the country in such condition that methods of recovery used in previous periods of depression were useless.

He had seen it as

. . . an emergency that went to the roots of our agriculture, our commerce and our industry; it was an emergency that had existed for a whole generation in its underlying causes and for three and one-half years in its visible effects. It could be cured only by a

complete reorganization and a measured control of the economic structure.

Yet, as he faced the tasks of the coming months, the country was still divided on his general policy as on no political issue since 1861. The proposals it was feared he would make were so divergent from the action of previous administrations and had been so lacking in development in his campaign utterances that the atmosphere of fear, in being dispelled, was followed by one of constant suspense and growing distrust. . . .

The New Deal that was . . . launched in the first hundred days of his administration was, as the President saw it, "a satisfactory combination of the Square Deal and the New Freedom . . . the fulfilment of the progressive ideas expounded by Theodore Roosevelt of a partnership between business and government and also of the determination of Woodrow Wilson that business should be subjected, through the power of government, to drastic legal limitations against abuses."

The President felt, furthermore, that:

In any event, the overwhelming majority of the business men in May, 1933, were entirely willing to go along with a great cooperative movement directed by the Government and working towards the elimination of the costly practices of the past.

There had been a swing of a large number of conservatives to the Roosevelt standard. They were being hospitably received and legislation of importance had been revised "in the light of the experience and opinion of men who work in the financial districts of the great cities." The boom support and stock market speculation of the 'twenties was thus in a way matched by the 'risks" taken on the New Deal by the American people as a whole.

The financial and industrial groups were actually the first to be rescued by the New Deal, which in the perspective of history must stand as the substitution of "government inflation, risk, experiment, and, indeed, speculation, for almost complete private responsibility in this respect . . . substitution . . . initiated and progressively developed at the request, or with the connivance, of powerful leaders in banking, industry, agriculture, and labor organizations. . . ."

Ultimately a day by day—not to say hour by hour—account of the events of 1933 will bring to the reader as near a reproduction as it is possible to furnish. It will be false to the truth, however, if it does not convey the sense of emergency, the feeling of desperate need, the determination that the will to live should be expressed in ceaseless activity.

By June 16, a Congress that had done the President's bidding toward relief, recovery—and reform—adjourned. That the response to this program had been varied was to be expected. On the whole, however, the country gave approval of action in all of these fields while waiting the degree of success that would attend it. Irrespective of the effects to be seen in labor, farming, and industry, it was clear—even in June—that the government of the United States had taken an advanced position.

In this, the aides to the President had been far more aggressive than any group in the Congress, even though individuals in both Senate and House—some of long experience in legislation of this kind—gave enthusiastic support. The President's personal advisers, who played an important part in the early months of the administration, were clearly working toward legislative and administrative action in three fields of great interest to

elements that had given support to the Democratic ticket—the farmer, the laborer, and the small business man so dependent upon loans and an active market.

Even as early as mid-April there was, however, restiveness among the more experienced members of Congress, who declared that speed had already resulted in ill-considered legislation. A group of Republican members of Congress issued a statement to the effect that the administration's inflation legislation "violates the most elementary principles of sound monetary credit and financial policies. It is better designed to defeat than to promote business recovery.". . .

The primary result of what his critics called "tinkering" with the currency was the furtherance of a "profound monetary revolution" by which, under cover of necessity, President Roosevelt was able to accomplish what radicals for generations had demanded. The devaluation of saved income, both of institutions and of individuals, Bryan had called for, as had the "silverites" up to 1930. Roosevelt's was revolutionary action under cover of law and was a blow intended to alter, in a fundamental way, the financial structure which had been built up by those who had hitherto dominated finance in the United States, not only in private but in public life.

This, accomplished as part of the recovery program, was in fact an evidence that the reform purposes of the President and his liberal advisers were dictating the new national policy. Control of the nation would be taken out of the hands of the bankers and placed in the hands of those who had seized control of the government under cover of a general mandate from the people. The President, guided and advised by groups convinced of the necessity of remaking the financial structure of the nation and backed by subservient Congressional majorities, was in truth remaking by executive order this financial structure not only in his own time but for the future. . . .

On the whole, despite the setbacks, uncertainties, and utter confusion of the summer and autumn months, the year 1933 witnessed a restoration of confidence in the future of the United States. All proposals that had been adopted were presented in a light to relate them in some degree to approved American practice and long-term improvements urged by American progressives.

It had been pointed out early in the spring that the President had done more "to start the nation toward a socialist order . . . than all the agitation carried on by all the avowedly socialist agents in our national history. . . . It is a new United States toward which Mr. Roosevelt is directing the nation." Much was made by critics of the fervent declarations of New Dealers that they were at last "rearranging existing society."

A thoughtful reader comes to an amazing conclusion in considering the rapid establishment of the new program. A group of intimates of the President, although changing personnel from time to time, is seen to have exercised tremendous power in a goverment, not of laws or of men but of ideas. Under cover of the President's name and backed by all of the power residing in the executive office, these men for a time not only formulated an economic program but imposed it, in all its ever-changing aspects, upon the people of the United States. Those who still say, "It can't happen here," should re-examine what happened to the United States when

President Franklin D. Roosevelt and his well-meaning advisers took over in 1933. The President who had exercised his power was to be given repeated endorsement by the people in whose name he had done it. . . .

Perhaps the question on which there was most discussion arose out of the assertion of a new role of government in caring for the interests of labor, of the farmer, of industry, and indeed of finance. Was it possible to plan for a continuance of capitalism under such an assumption of control and responsibility by the government? It appeared that in a world much concerned with the appeals of fascism and communism, a major modification of capitalism, in any important respect, was a serious matter. . . .

A long-standing query emerged more and more distinctly in discussion of the people at large. Were the traditional practices of American democracy going to survive the crisis of panic-depression followed by the administration program of recovery? Judging by the assurances of the President, Americans were to have a greater democracy and more extensive care for the masses of men.

Many thought and said, however, that the proposals made by the President were too slight to affect seriously the appalling deficiencies in social and economic democracy that had been revealed. Change must go further than had been proposed. Move quickly, they said, for the old American system is dead!

Amid the loud assertions of advocates of all brands of radicalism and the subdued protest of those who still felt that a conservative approach was now possible because the immediate crisis had passed, scant attention was given a question which in the long run was to have more significance than any. It was this: Could a program, based upon an appeal for increasing democratic process and greater social justice—relying upon widespread belief in the soundness of the popular will—be harmonized with the demands and needs of the modern industrial world? Could a program long called for, demanding experts in government and a truly informed electorate, be salvaged from the emotionalism that accompanied the early experiments of the New Deal?

In a reasoned survey of the status of the New Deal, Charles A. Beard found that, inasmuch as a long democratic tradition put first of all care for and interest in the people, the American background for the actions of the administration was clear enough. He concluded, however, "The tradition has been altered, of course, by an influx of ideas imported from the Old World.". . .

As the nation moved into the second year of the New Deal, Mr. Roosevelt felt that the restoration of confidence throughout the country had continued as a result of the fact that the executive and legislative arms of the government had proved themselves willing and able to take care of pressing problems. These problems continued to appear to him as the care of the suffering in the depression; second, erection of means whereby recurrence of this situation would be prevented; and third, steps to rebuild the bases of social justice. To substantiate this point of view, the President felt that statistics proved his contention, and he was proud of the legislation comprising reforms.

Those who opposed the President in his interpretation of what had happened repeatedly pointed out that reform tended to jeopardize recovery, in that it upset previous ways of thinking and acting and led to uncertainty as to the future. The President retorted that permanent recovery would demand a real readjustment of the economic system, which had tended to "concentrate power in the hands of a few." He was eager to assert that reforms would destroy control by a few, and cited speculation in securities and exploitation of labor as examples of the evils residing in such control.

Franklin Roosevelt did not originate attacks on selfish interests. There was a long line of practitioners of this method of political advancement. Yet at the conclusion of a review of legislation initiated by the executive and of his own more conspicuous utterances, he said:

I do not indict all business executives, all labor leaders, all editors, all lawyers. But I do indict the ethics of many of them and I indict those citizens whose easy consciences condone such wrong-doing. . . .

Vision is an essential in all service—some quality of the mind which is never satisfied with things as they are—some quality that achieves an immediate objective and proceeds forthwith to gain the next. It is only the cynic whom I have just described as a poor citizen who will suggest that the man or woman of vision is "impractical." The idealist is not of necessity a wretched executive. Some of the greatest administrators are people who are constantly seeking better things for mankind.

The President at this time stated that he was "fortunate in the unselfish loyalty and help given me by those like Howe and McIntyre and Early and Moley whose varied services I call upon at any hour of the day or night." Widespread rumor as to who was included in this group or trio of groups occupied the minds of many who at the time failed to perceive that the President's was a "personal" government which was certainly not new in the world, and which transcended even formal Presidential appointments.

Mr. Hull was the "idealist" whom the President had placed in the State Department, but it was not even the Secretary of State on whom the President relied for his foreign policy. Nor were the President's advisers chosen from any body of "experts" that would have been recognizable as such in the preceding administration. Nor was the Democratic party organization the source of Presidential advice. No progressives of either party were continuously influential in Presidential decisions.

A new element had come to power in the United States. It was vaguely termed a "brains trust" yet it included men of such diverse interest that a practical concern for "results" was perhaps the only unifying element in what Raymond Moley called the "card file" in Franklin Roosevelt's memory. Ideas and imagination were the qualifications for those who were associated with the President in any advisory capacity.

Although his associates changed constantly, the President moved, as most of the powerful leaders of the world have always done, through personal avenues of accomplishment. Much has been written of the men who surrounded the President and of their conjectured influence upon him. The evidence indicates that, though seeking the knowledge and views of countless individuals, the President made his own decisions and did not reveal to anyone what piece of information, expressed view, or attitude of others turned the scale.

The "feeling" of the period when the New Deal had passed its early crisis and there was a growing conviction that the greatest opportunity ever offered social reformers was in the grasp of those in office, is revealed in theater director Eva Le Gallienne's second autobiographical volume, *With a Quiet Heart*. Here is included the record of a conversation with Harry Hopkins following a dinner at the White House at which President Roosevelt and Miss Le Gallienne had discussed the possibility of her heading a National Theater Division of the W.P.A.

"Dear Miss LeGallienne," said Mr. Hopkins, "you should learn to play politics." After Miss Le Gallienne had replied that she had never learned to do this and was not sure that she wished to, Hopkins continued, "If you would just learn to play politics, you could get millions out of the old man."

Mr. Roosevelt's problem, throughout 1933 and 1934, was to direct the current of relief legislation in such a manner as to withstand attacks from extremists. But as he "gave in" to win support of the radicals, he faced full attack from the conservatives of all parties. The masses of the people—neither radical nor conservative—had for a long time demanded national solution of national problems heightened by the depression, and they submitted to the regulatory features of the President's recovery program because it seemed to be the result of their own demands.

In his basic conception of his function, the President had long since made clear that he thought of himself as representing all the people. But this in fact meant, in terms of policy or vote getting, reaching certain segments of the people. It was obvious that some he could not reach or did not wish to reach.

These included the lawbreakers either great or small, of whom in the circumstances of a speculating, bootlegging era there were thought to be many. The President did not address himself to the "privileged classes." Nor could he persuade the much larger number habitually adhering to the Republican party. Large numbers of conservative Democrats, particularly in the South, likewise refused to fall under his spell.

It followed that the President could attack many elements and in doing so would be acting for "the people." Surely *they* would be united in favor of the prosecution of lawbreakers. *They* would agree on restrictions upon privilege. *They* would enthusiastically support change of the rules making for wider use of the resources of the nation on behalf of the masses. In the very circumstances of the case, although President of the United States, he appeared to the people primarily as a fighter, a crusader—rather than as administrator and executive.

Yet in his relations with the Congress, particularly in matters of patronage but also in moves concerning legislation, the President displayed increasingly the adroitness of an experienced politician.

In judging the means he used, as well as his purpose, the distinction between recovery and reform is unreal. It is clear from both his statements and his actions that he would "recover" and "reform" by attacking abuses. His entire approach was based upon the proposition that the government, that is, the people, was strong enough to do anything necessary.

The government, in their name, could close the banks; it could reopen the banks for business; it could prosecute lawbreakers; it could build public works. If the government were to do these things and were to be all-powerful and able to plan for the future, as well as act from day to day, it must be supported. The

government in this conception was the *people*.

Thus, the government, that is, the people, must keep private enterprise actively and vigorously at work. In short, the economic life of the nation must be productive in order that taxation would be possible to pay the costs. It was therefore quite right to assert, as was so often done, that the administration, the President, and the people believed in private enterprise.

The tasks envisaged by the administration, in recovery and in reform, could not be accomplished by private agencies. It was inconceivable that national recovery and national reform could be accomplished by any other means than by a powerful aggressive government backed by the people. Moreover, a careful distinction was made that in the United States the people chose to do this. The American people, through their representatives, did it willingly....

Had Mr. Roosevelt ceased to be President in 1934, it is safe to assume that the New Deal would have disintegrated rapidly. Both the great party organizations were controlled by men who were disposed to move slowly and not take too seriously the demands of radicals for drastic reform of the whole system. Progressive programs had risen to widespread influence in this year of change.

This was not because the people had elected progressives to Congressional office in 1932. With the coming to the Presidency of Mr. Roosevelt, a union of forces for a time gave to his leadership a semblance of realization of the demands of such forerunners as the Populists and the Progressives and insurgents within both of the great parties.

A test of this in the elections of 1934, without the appeal of Mr. Roosevelt himself, would have brought prompt division of the Democrats into three if not four factions; of the Republican party into at least two factions. A strong popular movement, under the leadership of Huey Long, thus might have taken minority control of the Congress. It was the leadership of Franklin Roosevelt which prevented the development of this dangerous possibility.

Moreover, under his leadership in preparation for the tests of 1934, the call was continued for action on problems of agriculture and labor and, particularly, on social security. As the event proved, the main issue in the Congressional elections of 1934 came to be proposals for social security. The dominant public feeling was one of deep gratitude to Mr. Roosevelt for his leadership in what appeared to be national recovery in the spring and summer of 1933.

This first national opportunity for a record of popular response, which was afforded by the Congressional elections of 1934, brought from the President's point of view an overwhelming endorsement. The 60 Democrats in the Senate were increased to 65, thus reducing the Republicans to 25 with 2 Independents. The gain of a dozen Democrats in the House brought their number to 322, as against 102 Republicans and 10 Independents.

Despite the attack within his own party membership, as well as from the Republicans, the vote did seem to show that a great majority of the people supported the President in his conception of his duty to them. If so great a majority be given to a program already in action, was it not clear that the majority favored the next step in the program proposed?

The President had prepared the way for this view when he wrote:

Apart from phrases and slogans, the important thing to remember is, I think, that the change in our policy is based upon a change in the attitude and the thinking of the American people—in other words, that it is based upon the growing into maturity of our democracy; that it proceeds in accordance with the underlying principles that guided the framers of our Constitution; that it is taking form with the general approval of a very large majority of the American people; and finally, that it is made with the constant assurance to the people that if at any time they wish to revert to the old methods that we have discarded, they are wholly free to bring about such a reversion by the simple means of the ballot box. An ancient Greek was everlastingly right when he said, "Creation is the victory of persuasion and not of force." The New Deal seeks that kind of victory. . . .

It follows that the President's leadership was essential—and that everyone accepted the fact. It followed also that, if he were to hold together the movement that he had led thus far, he would turn not right, but increasingly left. Such a development would insure success in the Congress—and probably in the nation in the election of 1936.

"That he is entitled to full credit for inducing recovery" could be said by Walter Lippmann in early 1934 as "demonstrably certain."

Yet a British critic observed that "In thus pinning their faith to the hem of the garments of a superman, the American people in 1933 were reacting to the World Crisis in somewhat the same fashion as their German and Italian and Russian contemporaries."

But an American publishing *The New Dealers* under the pseudonym of "Unofficial Observer" wrote with keener insight

The essence of the peaceful revolution which has begun under Roosevelt is that it is a new deal and not a free-for-all. . . .

For the New Deal is a laughing revolution.

It is purging our institutions in the fires of mockery, and it is led by a group of men who possess two supreme qualifications for the task: common sense and a sense of humor.

It was said by the President that the people had nothing to fear but fear itself. This was primarily a call upon the individual to reassert his manhood. As the event proved, however, it was a suggestion that he might be saved by efforts other than his own. Presently he was assured that he *need* not fear, because his government would take care of him.

In this atmosphere of dependence, the American people easily gave over powers to the President. Millions were voted for the unemployed. Men co-operated in caring for themselves as they cared for their fellow citizens! This attitude of dependence—of itself working incalculable harm to the sturdy mind of America —was accompanied by cynicism and crass materialism. Much has been made of the iniquities of the industrial and financial world. Less has been said of the general attitude of distrust, envy, and disillusionment among the American people as a whole at this time. Too little, furthermore, has been said of the underlying feeling that enabled a people emerging from serious financial crisis to acclaim the repeal of the Eighteenth Amendment. . . .

Had the President chosen, now that the crisis was past, to turn "right," in the phrase of the day, it is absolutely certain that no leadership existent in the Congress could have commanded a national following for a program of social reform or economic change. If the President did not push reform, no one in Congress would do so. There were aspirants for opportunity to *lead*, but none of real competence. Not one, not even Huey Long, Senator from Louisiana, had the power.

Despite Mr. Roosevelt's apparent stand for a policy in advance of Mr. Hoover's, when the President now turned to dealing directly with the problem of insecurity in finance and the problem of social security, he found himself less eagerly followed.

The continuance of a program of government help for unemployment was apparently the most unorthodox of all his plans. It reflected the point of view and purpose of great numbers of social workers, but it certainly did not reflect the convictions of those who felt that government must pay its own way.

In due time, when all the materials are available and when years of research and analysis have carefully arranged the narrative of events, it will be possible to see with reasonable finality how the program of the New Deal was formulated, and why it was planned thus. At present this much can be said:

The President placed himself actively at the head of those who held that government is all-powerful; that it must act for the interests of the people as a whole; that it must convince them it so acts; and that the way to do this is to recognize divergent economic interests, and by arrangement, compromise, and even authoritarian control, to compel them to work together. . . .

The sessions of the Seventy-third Congress, which concluded in June of 1934, had made amply apparent to all who would see that two aspects of the legislative program associated with the New Deal were now coming to stand forth as all-important. One of these was full acceptance of the idea of vast federal expenditures contributing speedy recovery. The other was the growing satisfaction, at least among those in public office, at the large amount of patronage available and the increasing number of persons dependent upon federal subsidy.

The program of relief and recovery would in the nature of things cost billions. Inasmuch as no steps had yet been taken to deal effectively with the tax structure, it was apparent that this method of conducting government must rest upon the broad basis of borrowing. The free acceptance of this fact, not of particular interest to the public as a whole, was of vital concern to all those engaged in private enterprise.

A sense of insecurity and uncertainty as to the future was of course particularly felt by those interests in the financial and industrial world concerned with public utilities. The program of the administration embodied in the T.V.A. and the explanations of its purpose clearly foreshadowed extension of governmental activity in this field.

Mr. Hoover repeatedly warned that the greatest danger in planning and regimentation lay in decline of the representative body and undue reliance on bureaucracy. "We cannot extend the mastery of government over the daily life of the people," Mr. Hoover contended, "without somewhere making it master of people's souls and thoughts."

It was clear by this time that the American people had set forth upon an unaccustomed and dimly discerned road to the future.

RAYMOND MOLEY (1886–   ) was the most
important member of FDR's initial "brains trust," the
group of advisers who assisted him in policymaking as
governor of New York and as President. Professor of
government at Columbia, then in 1933 assistant
secretary of state and general speechwriter and idea
man for FDR, Moley had a commanding position in the
First New Deal. But his disagreement with the trend
of Roosevelt's policies steadily increased, and by 1937
he was in open opposition as a magazine and
newspaper columnist. The following critique of New
Deal policies from 1935 to 1938 reflects the impact of
their swift evolution on a man whose political and
social values were those of the progressive era.*

Lost Directions

... By December, 1934, there was evidence that business was executing a slow and majestic upturn. Through that month Roosevelt worked with Hopkins over the details of a program for work relief which Harry had sold him—a program to supplant the dole and the jerry-built made-work of the preceding year and a half with planned and supervised projects.

In January Roosevelt asked Congress for $4,000,000,000, plus $880,000,000 from the previous year's unexpended balances, to pay for this program. But the request for this staggering sum was not disquieting, business-wise. For, both in his budget message and annual message of 1935, he made it plain that he wasn't committing himself to the policy of purposeless public spending and that he intended to bring the budget into balance as rapidly as possible.

Even more important, the tone of his messages early that winter was conciliatory and friendly....

On January 4, 1935, he said to the country :"It is not empty optimism that moves me to a strong hope in the coming year. We can, if we will, make 1935 a genuine period of good feeling."

Yet the year 1935 was to prove a period of growing bitterness, of gradual insistence by the President upon the passage of such a gorge of indigestible measures that the New Deal itself was completely transformed.

* From *After Seven Years* by Raymond Moley, New York: Harper & Row, Publishers, Copyright, 1939, by Raymond Moley. Reprinted by permission of Brandt and Brandt.

This metamorphosis was the result of no single factor. True, it was always potentially implicit in Roosevelt's psychology. But its substantiation, its actual emergence from the cocoon of potentiality, was not inevitable. Except for the interaction of a half dozen circumstances between February and June, it might never have happened. These circumstance were:

1. The continuation of intemperate attacks upon him.
2. The continuation of the "needling" process by his own associates.
3. The irritation that comes from overwork and overstrain, which led him to resent the somewhat greater independence of the new Congress.
4. The immediately resultant fact that he began to get himself into positions from which it was difficult to retreat, to commit himself irrevocably to measures which, at first, he had accepted only tentatively.
5. The series of adverse Supreme Court decisions during those months, culminating in the invalidation of the N.I.R.A., which convinced him that the Supreme Court majority was out to destroy what he had accomplished.
6. The growing political strength of Huey Long.

It is necessary to elaborate.

Undeniably, there were a number of unjustifiable attacks upon Roosevelt, in meetings of various businessmen's associations that spring. This wasn't always the fault of the organization before which the inflammatory words were uttered. But it was Roosevelt's impulse always to blame the organization for having permitted violent critics of his policies to appear. Coupled with this was a growing petulance about newspaper criticism. More often than not, during those months, when I came into his bedroom, he would comment angrily about the papers he had read over his breakfast. This paper had said "something untrue," that paper was being "consistently unfair," another paper was being "run by a publisher who exploits his men."

Finally, and particularly provoking, was a silly practice that flourished in many business quarters—the practice of passing around stories about the President or his family that were intended to be funny and were always derogatory. Almost all Presidents have been the butts of asinine jokes, but it's hard to remember a more vicious crop of them than that spring produced. . . .

But the "needlers" were by no means the only irritants. There were others—men, such as Harold Ickes, who had been in the political minority so long before 1933 that they were slow to recapture the dignity and confidence the public expects of those who are parts of the ruling group. These men, used to the practices of political guerrilla warfare, accustomed to sudden sallies and hasty retreats, found it hard to sit calmly in the seats of power and smile at attacks in outlying provinces. This was the explanation for their extreme sensitiveness, their unnecessary and undignified replies to small-fry criticism, their continuous stirring up of the President by these replies.

Imagine, if you can, the effect of all this upon a President who was finding Congress a good deal talkier and balkier than its predecessor. There were two clear reasons why F.D.R.'s wishes carried less weight with the 74th Congress than with the 73rd: most of the patronage had been given out, and the administration itself, rather than Congress alone, had to face an election in 1936. But as the days passed, in April and May, the

President thought of these things less and less It was easier, for reasons that will appear, to think that waves of reactionary propaganda were sweeping over the national legislature.

Early in January, 1935, F.D.R. told me of his legislative plans. They weren't at all formidable. He wanted social-security legislation, a modest holding-company act, a work-relief program, a merchant-marine act, a revised N.I.R.A., and one or two odds and ends. That was all.

What actually happened that spring was this:

1. To prepare the social-security act, the President had set up a Cabinet Committee. This Committee then established a research organization and asked a considerable number of citizens, including myself, to serve as an advisory committee. The advisory committee considered every aspect of the problem with care and made a series of recommendations to the Cabinet Committee, which promptly threw out many of them. The bill that was finally sent to Congress was so largely the result of an attempt to compromise irreconcilable views that frank observers recognized it for the mess it was. The two responsible committees of Congress naturally began to overhaul it. Net result—a long and agonizing fight between its administration sponsors and Congress.

2. Late in February it developed that three distinct holding-company proposals had been prepared for the President's consideration— one by Corcoran and Cohen after conference with me, one by Walter M. W. Splawn of the I.C.C. at Sam Rayburn's request (F. D. R. had, of course, suggested that Rayburn think about such legislation), and one by Herman Oliphant and Robert H. Jackson of Morgenthau's Department. These were progressively drastic—the last absolutely destroying holding companies. Frankfurter, Cohen, Corcoran, and I all urged that the President accept the moderate Cohen-Corcoran draft, but he in-

clined toward the stiffer proposals. In the end Cohen and Corcoran agreed to sharpen their pencils. The result was the "death-sentence" provision which neither they nor the President really expected to get through Congress, but which they intended to use for trading purposes. But in the course of the desperate struggle over the bill (in the Senate an attempt to remove the "death sentence" was defeated by only one vote) the President, Corcoran, and Cohen managed to sell themselves all they originally asked for. The two young men were in and out of the White House, day after day, night after night, reporting the progress of their campaign to "put the heat on" reluctant senators. Between them they generated enough indignation over the opposition to the bill to become the victims of their own strategy. The fight became a fight for all or nothing. *Aut Caesar aut nullus* was the mood of late spring.

3. Nothing was done, that spring, to devise more than halfway plans to reconstruct the N.I.R.A. The President merely suggested slight revisions and asked Congress for an extension of the N.I.R.A., which expired in June. This throwing-up of the presidential hands was the signal for a long, acrimonious wrangle before the Finance Committee of the Senate.

4. Senator Wagner's Labor-Relations bill, which the President had no intention of supporting in January, developed unforeseen strength in Congress. As spring came on, the President faced the necessity of deciding whether he would accept it. By early June, partly because he needed the influence and votes of Wagner on so many pieces of legislation and partly because of the invalidation of the N.I.R.A., he flung his arms open and suddenly embraced the Wagner bill—whose palpable one-sidedness could have been eliminated then and there.

5. Meanwhile the Guffey Bituminous Coal bill, sponsored by John L. Lewis, came along. In May the President wisely refused to commit himself to it. On June 1st the United Mine Workers officials sent out strike orders. On June 4th, after the invalidation of the

N.I.R.A., Roosevelt pressed for the enactment of the bill. On July 6th in an effort to avert a walkout of the U.M.W., he urged the House subcommittee considering the bill not to permit doubts as to its constitutionality, "however reasonable, to block the suggested legislation."

What happened, in short, was that Roosevelt dumped into Congress' lap three major puzzles centering in the proposed security bill, the proposed N.I.R.A. extension, and the proposed holding-company bill; that he grew impatient with the long debate over them; and that, either to buttress his position or for trading purposes, he then let himself be committed to other pieces of legislation he orginally had no idea of demanding.

It was clear by early June, 1935, that he had bitten off far more than he could chew. But he was now in no mood to drop anything. His stubbornness was thoroughly aroused. The more sullen Congress grew over his "must" lists, the more positive he became of his rectitude. The ardor of his advocacy began to turn inward, feeding upon its own flame, enlarging and intensifying with every hint of opposition, every breath of criticism.

Still the situation might not have become explosive, but for Huey Long and the Supreme Court.

In the early spring of 1935 the Democratic leaders began to get an acute attack of jitters about the apparently growing political strength of the Kingfish. It is probable that they overestimated both the shrewdness and the political future of the blatant, picturesque, arm-flailing Louisiana dictator to the same extent that smug Easterners who dismissed him as a mountebank underestimated them. Certainly those in Washington who called his "Share-the-Wealth" movement "the greatest threat to Franklin Roosevelt and his New Deal" had lost all perspective....

F.D.R. began to doubt whether Huey's followers could be weaned away by logical argument. Perhaps it would be necessary to woo some of Long's support by making a counteroffer. One evening in midspring F.D.R. actually used the phrase "steal Long's thunder" in conversation with me and two other friends of his.

In the midst of all this the Supreme Court began to deliver one blow after another to the New Deal. On January 7th section 9 (c) of the N.I.R.A. was declared unconstitutional. On May 6th the Railroad Retirement Act was overthrown. On May 27th the President's removal of Commissioner Humphrey from the Federal Trade Commission was severely chastised, the Frazier-Lemke amendments to the Bankruptcy Act were declared unconstitutional, and, in the famous Schechter case, the code-making provisions of the N.I.R.A. were invalidated.

This series of reverses convinced F.D.R. that the Court majority was the implacable enemy of all change, that unless its basic philosophy was overhauled all that he had done would be undone.

A fairly just deduction was that the Supreme Court decision in the Schechter case delivered Roosevelt from one of the most desperate administrative muddles he ever confronted and gave him the opportunity to start over, in this field, with a fairly clean slate. Unfortunately, once the slate had been cleaned, Roosevelt seemed unable to make up his mind what to write on it....

It was at that point that the two impulses—the impulse to strike back at his critics and the impulse to "steal Long's thunder"— flowed together and crystallized. He remembered something

—a scheme that had come from the Treasury back in February—a scheme, it suddenly dawned on him, that might have been devised for the very purposes he had in mind. ...

On a June night in 1935 the President showed Felix Frankfurter and myself a draft message from the Treasury recommending the taxation of "unwieldy and unnecessary corporate surpluses," a heavy inheritance and gift tax, a sharp increase in surtaxes on incomes above $50,000, and a graduated corporation-income tax. The proposal as a whole was declared a revision of the existing tax system because it operated "to the unfair advantage of a few" and because "social unrest and a deepening sense of unfairness" required a "wider distribution of wealth."

This was the "soak-the-rich" scheme—designed to embarrass and annoy a few wealthy individuals, win the support of the "Share-the-Wealth" adherents, and "discourage" bigness in business.

To say that I was appalled by the satisfaction with which F.D.R. informed me that he intended to send this message to Congress (he added blithely, "Pat Harrison's going to be so surprised he'll have kittens on the spot") is to fall over backwards with restraint. ...

The best I could do was to persuade Roosevelt to narrow the range of the graduated corporate-income tax he insisted upon recommending and to dissuade him from asking for more than a study of the surplus-tax proposal. For the rest, he was adamant. The sense of regaining the whip hand gave him the first buoyant, cheerful moment he had known for weeks. He airily dismissed most of our objections.

The message was sent to Congress on June 19th.

It was on that day the split in the Democratic party began.

The message stunned the Congressional leaders. Those, like Pat Harrison, who felt that party loyalty compelled them to support it, bled inwardly. Many, cut to the quick by the peremptory tone of the message, said bitterly they'd "go down the line" this time, but that they'd be damned if they ever would again under like circumstances. Others announced in the cloakrooms that, party loyalty or no party loyalty, they were going to turn the scheme inside out and show of what it was made. ...

An uproarious drive to override most of the President's tax recommendations got under way in the House. Businessmen wailed that the President must be pursuing a private vendetta against his old friends of Groton and Harvard, that dangerous communists were scuttling in and out of his presence like messenger boys in a broker's office (ante 1929). Hot-headed administration subordinates talked of the need for "clipping business' wings." The President expressed amazement that capitalists did not understand that he was their savior, the only bulwark between them and revolution. The battle-to-the-death spirit was unmistakable.

I began to wonder whether Roosevelt had begun to see his program as an end in itself, rather than as a means to an end; whether he wasn't beginning to feel that the proof of a measure's merit was the extent to which it offended the business community; whether he wasn't substituting, for the attempt to coordinate the economic life of the nation, a program of *divide et impera;* whether the search for the Holy Grail of a just national economy wasn't being transformed into a strafing expedition. ...

"There's one issue in this campaign,"

Roosevelt had announced in May. "It's myself.". . .

That was the essence of the campaign of 1936.

It asked no "great and solemn referendum." It did not undertake to register a national decision or even a series of national decisions on future policies. It did not ask the voters to sanction a specific course of governmental action. It invited only an expression of faith in a man.

By dint of much wishful thinking a number of doubtful Democrats were able to persuade themselves that, after the election, Mr. Roosevelt would suddenly be transformed. The responsibilities of his second term, they argued, would impose on him a less "political," less opportunistic, more measured administration of his office and a more generous attitude toward those who sometimes disagreed with him.

Yet it seemed to me that the effect of the campaign and the election would be the precise opposite. There was nothing in Roosevelt's career to indicate that success would make him more judicious. And the danger of his belief that he was the embodiment rather than the servant of progressivism was intensified a thousandfold by the nature of his appeal.

The campaign began quietly enough, with trips to various projects where the use to which federal money had been put could be skillfully dramatized. By October its theme appeared less delicately. It was nothing more or less than an attempt to identify Roosevelt's objectives with the objectives of as many other people as possible. The new, organized army of the unemployed, mobilized Northern negroes, conservative Republican farmers from the corn belt,

the growing membership of the C.I.O., Norman Thomas' vanishing army of orthodox Socialists, Republican progressives and Farmer-Laborites, Share-the-Wealthers, single-taxers, Sinclairites, Townsendites, Coughlinites, the medicine men from a thousand campfires— all were invited to give their allegiance to the Democratic candidate. They were to follow him because each saw, or thought he saw, the moon of his desire floating in the beneficent sky of Roosevelt's humanitarian aspirations. A mystic bond of sympathy was being created between Roosevelt and his audiences. . . .

But vast audiences cannot be electrified by the repetition of vague promises. And it was impossible to be explicit about future plans because there were no future plans. Since the statesman had left the orator in possession of the field, only one course was possible. New and more thrilling flourishes were required as the October days passed. The bond that words had spun, words had to make incandescent. Roosevelt and his listeners had to be fused by a flow of sensations— by hope, fear, gratitude, hate.

The speeches through October became increasingly emotional. So did the audiences. So did the speaker. For he had succumbed completely to the heady spell he was creating. That became unmistakable on the night of October 31, 1936.

There could be no question, by that time, of how overwhelming his victory would be. His political opponents were at his feet. His battle was won. It was the moment when a referee stops the fight and mercifully announces a technical knockout. That referee should have been Roosevelt's instinct for moderation. Had it been operating, these words could not have been spoken:

"We had to struggle with the old

enemies of peace—business and financial monopoly, speculation, reckless banking, class antagonism, sectionalism, war profiteering.

"They had begun to consider the Government of the United States as a mere appendage to their own affairs. We know now that Government by organized money is just as dangerous as Government by organized mob.

"Never before in all our history have these forces been so united against one candidate as they stand today. They are unanimous in their hate of me—and I welcome their hatred.

"I should like to have it said of my first Administration that in it the forces of selfishness and of lust for power met their match. I should like to have it said of my second Administration that in it these forces met their master."

Thoughtful citizens were stunned by the violence, the bombast, the naked demagoguery of these sentences. No one who has merely read them can half know the meaning conveyed by the cadences of the voice that uttered them.

Roosevelt was the master of a great deal that night. But he was subject to a master, too. He was the plaything of his own desire for effect. . . .

Roosevelt had been reelected by a huge aggregation of hopelessly incompatible elements. He was not going to be able to discover the least common denominator of the wishes of all the groups that supported him because there was no such thing. Their unity rested not in attachment to each other, or even to him, but in the belief that Roosevelt had promised to provide an abundant life in accordance with each of a score of contradictory specifications. Such a victory carried the seeds of its own defeat. But Roosevelt could not be expected

to see that. The size of his majority, in itself, would produce that overweening confidence that would blind him to the dangers of his situation. Now more than ever, he would be certain that he could reconcile the irreconcilable, certain of his infallibility. . . .

The Court Disapproves, Roosevelt called the 1935 volume of his collected papers, and the 1936 volume, *The People Approve.*

That no such appeal from the Court to the voters as these titles suggest was made in 1936 is a matter of record. Still these titles afford a significant clue to Roosevelt's psychology. No doubt his firm belief, or rather his firm will to believe, that the people of this country had given him a general cease-and-desist order to execute against all who challenged him led him to his greatest defeat.

The announcement of the plan to pack the Supreme Court caught wholly off guard a public and a Congress lulled by three months of exquisite calm. Roosevelt's pronouncements in the course of his good-will trip to South America would not have frightened the birds of St. Francis. His quiet message to Congress asked cooperation from the Supreme Court in a manner to which even the sternest constitutionalist could not object. His second inaugural speech was peaceable and statesmanlike. For the most part, the man-sobered-by-great-victory tableau was accepted without reserve. Only a few lynx-eyed observers pointed to the jokers in the Reorganization message of January 12, 1937. Only a few people who knew the President very well indeed wondered, privately, just how and when the quiet would be shattered this time.

The stunning answer came on February 5th.

The President's bare attempt to pack the Court was not at all concealed by his arguments that the Court needed enlargement because it was inefficient, because age was related to inefficiency, and because age and conservatism went hand in hand. It was recognized at once for what it was—a plan to provide in advance for Supreme Court approval of whatever legislative reforms Roosevelt happened to espouse, a plan to enable Roosevelt to control the Court. . . .

There's no need to review the complicated and fascinating history of the six months' battle over Court packing. As everyone knows, it ended well, and will doubtless insure the people of the United States against any similar presidential attempt so long as our democratic republic lasts. It's relevant here chiefly as the overt expression of the mood I had feared and resisted for over a year. . . .

It was one of the most revealing aspects of the Court fight that at no time in its course did the President indicate, except in terms so general as to be meaningless, the kind of economic reform that his "reinvigorated" Court was supposed to approve. That he didn't because he had still not resolved the indecision which began with the N.I.R.A.'s invalidation in May, 1935, seemed a reasonable assumption. But it remained for the onset of the "recession" of 1937-38 to confirm it publicly. The crisis that set in during September, 1937, provided, in fact, the most spectacular demonstration of presidential irresolution since the days when Hoover had stood nonplused before some of the same ugly economic realities.

For seven long months Roosevelt blew hot and cold, delayed, temporized, played his subordinates against each other, alternately echoed and contradicted them,

while business indices sagged, unemployment rose, and Washington officialdom fell into a rancorous, raucous, many-sided quarrel. . . .

The crisis of indecision that became a matter of public knowledge in the autumn of 1937 cannot be understood except as an extension of what had gone before. I suppose it was significant that Roosevelt's formative years were coincidental with the growing ascendancy in American thought of William James' pragmatism. At any rate, in the realm of economics and politics, Roosevelt carried to its logical and perhaps tragic ultimate the philosophy of trial and error so joyously preached by James. I have never known a man so receptive to the new and unorthodox. During the critical years of 1932 and 1933 it was my most difficult job to see that he took the opportunity to examine skeptically the "plans" and devices that attracted his interest. Even so, the most extraordinary fragments of rejected ideas would remain in his mind to be played with, when time permitted, and, sometimes, as in the case of the "soak-the-rich" scheme, to be suddenly announced as settled policies.

This receptiveness to innovation was not in itself objectionable. On the contrary, it was this very quality in Roosevelt that made it possible for him to root out the economic shibboleths to which most of our best-advertised thinkers had stubbornly clung after 1929. It was this quality that made it possible for him to begin repairing, on a monumental scale, a system which a decade of abuse had left racked and broken.

The hitch came with Roosevelt's failure to follow through. Pragmatism requires the application of the test of utility or workableness or success. And by this Roosevelt refused to abide. He would launch an idea as an experiment, but, once it had been launched, he would not subject it to the pragmatic test. It became, in his mind, an expression of settled conviction, an indispensable element in a great, unified plan.

That Roosevelt could look back over the vast aggregation of policies adopted between March, 1933, and November, 1936, and see it as the result of a single, predetermined plan was a tribute to his imagination. But not to his grasp of economics. One had only to review the heterogeneous origins of the policies he had embraced by the time of his reelection, the varying circumstances, impulses, beliefs that had produced them, to guess at their substantive conflict and contradiction. . . .

If this aggregation of policies springing from circumstances, motives, purposes, and situations so various gave the observer the sense of a certain rugged grandeur, it arose chiefly from the wonder that one man could have been so flexible as to permit himself to believe so many things in so short a time. But to look upon these policies as the result of a unified plan was to believe that the accumulation of stuffed snakes, baseball pictures, school flags, old tennis shoes, carpenter's tools, geometry books, and chemistry sets in a boy's bedroom could have been put there by an interior decorator.

Or, perhaps it would be more apt to say that the unfolding of the New Deal between 1932 and 1937 suggested the sounds that might be produced by an orchestra which started out with part of a score and which, after a time, began to improvise. It might all hang together if there were a clear understanding between the players and the conductor as to the sort of music they intended to produce.

But nothing was more obvious than that some of the New Deal players believed that the theme was to be the funeral march of capitalism; others, a Wagnerian conflict between Good and Evil; and still others, the triumphant strains of the *Heldenleben.*

Yet what could be said of the conductor who emerged from such an experience and who announced that he and his orchestra had produced new and beautiful harmonies?

It was Roosevelt's insistence upon the essential unity of his policies that inevitably brought into question his understanding of economics. Except in terms of misunderstanding, there was no way to comprehend such phenomena as an attempt to rehabilitate the soft-coal business which proceeded without reference to simultaneous efforts to encourage the production of electricity through vast water-power projects. There was no other possible explanation for the slow blurring of the distinction between temporary and permanent economic policies, the retention of expedients designed to meet emergency problems, and the justification of such expedients on grounds quite unlike those which had warranted their initial employment. There was no other possible explanation for the two-and-a-half year indifference to the obstacles that thwarted a huge potential demand for additional houses and dammed up a potent force for stable economic recovery. So, too, there would be in 1939 no other possible explanation for the plea that the loss of dollar-devaluation powers would remove "the only check we have on . . . speculative operations" by the same President who, six years before, had announced that he knew of no way governments could check exchange speculation.

Underlying these and a host of other

incongruities were two misapprehensions which were basic.

The first centered in a failure to understand what is called, for lack of a better term, business confidence. . . .

In fact, the term "confidence" became, as time went on, the most irritating of all symbols to him. He had the habit of repelling the suggestion that he was impairing confidence by answering that he was restoring the confidence the public had lost in business leadership. No one could deny that, to a degree, this was true. The shortsightedness, selfishness, and downright dishonesty of some business leaders had seriously damaged confidence. Roosevelt's assurances that he intended to cleanse and rehabilitate our economic system did act as a restorative.

But beyond that, what had been done? For one thing, the confusion of the administration's utility, shipping, railroad, and housing policies had discouraged the small individual investor. For another, the administration's taxes on corporate surpluses and capital gains, suggesting, as they did, the belief that a recovery based upon capital investment is unsound, discouraged the expansion of producers' capital equipment. For another, the administration's occasional suggestions that perhaps there was no hope for the reemployment of people except by a share-the-work program struck at a basic assumption in the enterpriser's philosophy. For another, the administration's failure to see the narrow margin of profit on which business success rests—a failure expressed in an emphasis upon prices while the effects of increases in operating costs were overlooked—laid a heavy hand upon business prospects. For another, the calling of names in political speeches and the vague, veiled threats of punitive action all tore the fragile texture of credit

and confidence upon which the very existence of business depends. . . .

The second basic fault in the congeries of the administration's economic policies sprang from Roosevelt's refusal to make a choice between the philosophy of Concentration and Control and the philosophy of Enforced Atomization.

It was easy to see that the early New Deal, with its emphasis on agricultural and industrial planning, was dominated by the theory of Concentration and Control—by the beliefs that competition is justified only in so far as it promotes social progress and efficiency; that government should encourage concerted action where that best serves the public and competition where that best serves the public; that business must, under strict supervision, be permitted to grow into units large enough to insure to the consumer the benefits of mass production; that organized labor must likewise be permitted to grow in size but, like business, be held to strict accountability; that government must cooperate with both business and labor to insure the stable and continuous operation of the machinery of production and distribution.

But with the invalidation of the N.I.R.A., there was a shift in emphasis. And this shift took not the form of a complete repudiation of Concentration and Control, but of an endless wavering between it and the philosophy advocated by those Brandeis adherents, like Corcoran, who preached the "curse of bigness," the need for breaking up great corporations on the ground that their growth was the result of the desire for financial control rather than increased efficiency, the desirability of "atomizing" business in order to achieve a completely flexible competitive system which would work without much intervention by government. . . .

Roosevelt obviously clung to the belief that he could *blend* the two philosophies by persuasion and skillful compromise, though the evidence proving that he could merely *mix* them piled up through 1936 and the first half of 1937. And since, in this world, bitterness and distrust are as likely to arise from bewilderment as from inborn propensities, the indecision which had begun in May, 1935, in no small part contributed to the business collapse of 1937.

So the stage was set when the depression struck in September, 1937. And so began the noisy pulling and hauling in Washington between the advocates of budget balancing, the advocates of spending, the believers that the price fixing of monopolies had caused the contraction of business, and the believers that the uncertainty and confusion of administration policy had made impossible those long-term business plans which sustain employment and consumer purchasing power.

The reaction was a steadily deepening indecision.

In November, 1937, the President approved a speech by Secretary Morgenthau intended to reassure business because it committed the administration to stringent budget balancing.

In December, 1937, and January, 1938, the President acquiesced in a campaign launched by Corcoran, Cohen, Ickes, Hopkins, and Robert H. Jackson for the purpose of blaming the depression upon business. Jackson and Ickes at once began an oratorical "trust-busting" offensive—a series of bitter speeches, replete with references to "corporate earls," "corporate tentacles," and "aristocratic anarchy"—planned and partly prepared, according to Alsop and Kintner, by the young lawyers and economists Corcoran had welded into what he called his "well-integrated group" and into what Hugh Johnson characterized as "the janissariat."

On January 3, 1938, Roosevelt spoke, in one breath, of great corporations created "for the sake of securities profits, financial control, the suppression of competition and the ambition for power over others" and, in the next breath, announced, "We ask business and finance . . . to join their government in the enactment of legislation where the ending of abuses and the steady functioning of our economic system calls for government assistance."

On January 4th Roosevelt suggested that he would like to see businessmen and industrialists draw up chairs to a table with government representatives and work out a scheme to adjust production schedules to coincide with demand.

On January 8th the President denounced the "autocratic controls over the industry and finances of the country."

Through February and March the battle over policy, the effort to force a presidential decision dragged.

Governor Eccles of the Federal Reserve Board pleaded for pump priming and the removal of legislative and administrative constrictions—especially in the fields of labor and housing—that were blocking the normal course of business. Secretary Morgenthau harped on the need for a balanced budget. Jesse Jones of the R.F.C. campaigned for the repeal of the corporate-surplus tax. Donald Richberg urged a resumption of cooperative efforts to plan production. S.E.C. Commissioner John W. Hanes appealed for gestures reassuring to business. The Corcoran-Cohen-Hopkins-Ickes brigade, armed with memoranda provided by

Leon Henderson, economic adviser to the W.P.A., and by others of the "well-integrated group," planked day in and day out for a combined spending and antimonopoly campaign.

There were passionate arguments between many of these advisers, secret meetings in homes and offices to patch up alliances, dashes to Warm Springs where the President was vacationing late in March, importunate telephone calls, desperate and extravagant pleas for action.

It was April, with all business indices plummeting, before Roosevelt agreed, at last, to ask Congress for an investigation of monopolies and for a $3,012,000,000 spending program.

This move was hailed by the "well-integrated group" as the earnest of Roosevelt's complete conversion to their point of view.

In the sense that they had sold to him, together with the emergency program for spending, an elaborate philosophic rationalization of the inevitable, they had won a real victory. The rationalization, of which the most vociferous evangel was David Cushman Coyle, insisted that expenditures which returned dividends only in social benefit or esthetic pleasure were no less "assets" than those which paid dividends in taxable capacity, that a mounting deficit stimulated recovery. Corcoran's susceptibility to this strange and jumbled doctrine seemed to trace back to Brandeis' beliefs, expressed to me in detail in 1933, that private capital investment was virtually at an end because business could no longer find enough attractive opportunities for investment and that government must fill the void thus created. Roosevelt unquestionably embraced the doctrine as a handy way to justify a continuing budget unbalance for which he had excoriated Hoover during the campaign of 1932 and against which he had repeatedly pledged himself, up to January, 1937. But, aside from the reasons for the doctrine's adoption, it became, once adopted, a kind of pansophy—a scheme of universal wisdom. Embellishments appeared. Money must be "shoveled out," Corcoran remarked in private conversation. Roosevelt put it differently. In his budget message of 1939, he said that an indispensable factor in prosperity was government "investment" great enough to lift the national income to a point which would make tax receipts cover the new level of expenditure.

So far, the "conversion" was absolute.

But the claim that Roosevelt was won over to a policy of "antibigness" in April, 1938, did not stand up. True, the President, in a fiery message, prepared with the assistance of Corcoran, Cohen, Jackson, and others of the "well-integrated group," denounced monopoly. Yet he went no further than to ask for a thorough congressional study of "the concentration of economic power in American industry"—a study which was to go on for a year or two.

This request for a study was, certainly, the final expression of Roosevelt's personal indecision about what policy his administration ought to follow in its relations with business. The creation of the "monopoly" committee, or rather the Temporary National Economic Committee, merely relieved Roosevelt, for the moment, from the nagging of subordinates who, whatever the differences in their own economic philosophies, recognized that an administration which was of two minds on this all-important question would contradict itself into disaster.

It merely put off the adoption of a guiding economic philosophy. . . .

The *New Republic* first appeared in 1914 as the voice of advanced progressivism. In the 1930s it was one of the major periodicals of the American Left. The following survey of the later New Deal by the magazine's editors is dissatisfied with the administration's economic policies for precisely the reverse of Moley's reasons: its complaint is that the power of big business was not more thoroughly trammeled. But it finds much to commend in the social reforms of the Roosevelt administration—the new ventures that contributed so much to Moley's uneasiness.*

The New Deal in Review 1936–1940

Economic Recovery

What progress has the New Deal made since 1936 in fulfilling the economic promise of American life? Whatever else it may have done or not done, this subject is central, since it was the great economic collapse that brought the New Deal into power. . . .

In summary . . . we find that economic progress has not proceeded during the second term of the New Deal, though previous recovery gains have not been lost, except during the slumps of 1938 and the end of 1939. Income is still too low; unemployment far too great. The reason is not lack of business earnings. The chief trouble is lack of new invest-ment, especially in building. Governmental spending, and particularly governmental stimulation to housing, offered the brightest spot in the picture. The war has recently expanded the aircraft industry and a few others, but it has brought slackened demand as well for certain agricultural and other products, and on the whole it is negligible, so far, as a stimulus to our economy.

Fiscal Policy

Next only to the general economic conditions of the country, the fiscal policy of the New Deal comes in for the most blame or defense. Conservatives attack the recurring deficits and the growth of

* The editors of the *New Republic,* "The New Deal in Review 1936–1940," vol. 102 (May 20, 1940), pp. 687–708. © The New Republic.

the national debt. Thinking of the United States as if it were a single business enterprise or an individual, interested mainly in making profits or putting money in the bank, they are made uncomfortable by these things. The deficit is blamed for creating a lack of business confidence and so hampering expansion, and the eventual outcome is foreseen as either bankruptcy or intolerable taxation. Defenders of the government's policy make numerous points such as that the spending is necessary to relieve distress so long as business does not revive sufficiently, that much of it creates permanent values and so increases the real worth of the country, that business would be worse than it is if it were not for government spending, that as investment this spending helps fill the gap left by the lack of private investment. . . .

Recovery expenditures—including the agricultural-readjustment program as well as public works of all kinds and unemployment relief—grew rapidly between 1933 and 1937, or from $832,000,000 to $4,156,000,000. In Mr. Roosevelt's second administration, however, they have shown no increase. In 1938 they dropped to $3,238,000,000. In 1939 they were increased again to $4,570,000,000, but in 1940 it is estimated that they will be only $3,931,000,000, and the budget for the fiscal year 1941 puts them at $3,015,-000,000. It is an interesting observation that while economic recovery was most rapid—between 1933 and 1937—recovery expenditures were growing rapidly, that there were slumps when they were reduced in 1938 and 1940, and a revival in 1939 when they were increased. . . .

Few people realize that the only substantial increase in federal expenditures since 1936 has been that for the army and navy. National defense cost $633,-000,000 in 1933, $895,000,000 in 1937. Since then it has steadily grown, being $1,457,000,000 in 1940, and, according to budget estimates, will be $1,834,000,000 in 1941, or more than twice the figure of four years ago. This is more than was spent either on relief or on public works this year. We are turning from roads, flood control, housing and food for the unemployed to battleships, guns and planes. These things may be needed in the present state of the world, but they do not contribute so much to the establishment of a sound economy as expenditures of a different character. It is a question whether the conservatives who condemn the spending policy of the government would want to reduce money for defense, as they do want to reduce that used for social welfare. . . .

In our view, the administration is to be censured, not for spending, creating a deficit and increasing the national debt, but for adopting halfway measures in this regard and for not working out a well planned long-term spending policy. A governmental credit agency like the United States Housing Administration could, without great net expense to the taxpayers, increase current housing operations enormously, meet a real need and stimulate the lagging construction industry. A general solution of the railroad problem under government administration could open the way for large new investment in that industry. The chance for expansion of the power industry, under either private or public auspices, is enormous if rates are set low enough. A great opportunity for government is to act as a canal for new investment in productive enterprises—provided government can so reorganize and control these enterprises as to make for larger production at lower prices.

Economic Regulation

Aside from its spending policy, the New Deal has attempted to do something about our limping economy by regulation. The purpose has been twofold—to try to get it more into balance and so to stimulate activity, and to do justice to underpaid farmers and workers by giving them a larger share of what is produced. . . .

One of the main efforts of the Agricultural Adjustment Administration has been to increase the prices received by farmers, first by the domestic-allotment plan; then, when that was declared unconstitutional, indirectly by soil-conservation payments and other crop-limitation policies. All this time its efforts have been hampered by the fact that some of our most important crops depend on export markets, and these have been shrinking.

The index of prices received by farmers for their products stood at 146 in 1929 (the index being based at 100 for the average of the years 1909-14). It was more than cut in half by 1932, standing at 65. The early recovery efforts of the New Deal helped it to rise to 114 in 1936. In 1937 it went up another notch—to 121. Then it fell off again to 95 in 1938 and 93 in 1939. It has shown a slight rising tendency this year. Thus, in the last four years farm prices have not improved.

Meanwhile prices paid by the farmer for goods used in living and production have stayed fairly high. They were 153 in 1929, fell only to 107 in 1932, and came back to 124 in 1936 and 130 in 1937. In 1939 they were 120. In terms of price relationships, the farmer is better off than he was in 1929, much better off than in 1932, and not quite so well off as before the first World War.

The New Deal has been uncertain what to do about industrial prices and prices charged to consumers, though on the whole it is agreed by economists that many of them are too high—particularly the prices of capital goods like steel. . . .

The setting up of great public power projects under the TVA and elsewhere, with encouragement for public or coöperative distribution, and the work of the Rural Electrification Administration, have resulted in reduced rates and wider distribution of electricity. This result has been achieved almost entirely because of lower costs, brought about in private utilities by the stimulus of government competition. The REA reduction in cost of construction was from $1,500 or $1,800 a mile to about $800. Customers of agencies distributing TVA power use on the average 1,179 k.w.h. annually, as against about 850 for the nation as a whole. Their average cost was 2.14 cents per k.w.h. in 1938 as against 4.21 in the country. The TVA cost has kept on falling. . . .

The most ambitious attempt made by the government during the past four years to regulate wages and hours was the passage and administration of the Fair Labor Standards Act. The Department of Labor estimated that 12,290,000 employees came under the provisions of the act, and that of these 650,000 would receive wage increases because they were receiving less than 30 cents an hour, and 2,380,000 would be affected by a reduction of the standard working week to forty-two hours—either by a reduction of hours or by receiving overtime pay. During the first month after the forty-two-hour limit went into effect (in October, 1939) there was a decline of 1.3 percent from the previous month in average weekly hours in manufacturing, in spite of a slight increase in total employment. In a few industries, higher standards than the legal minima have been established under the law by advice of industry committees. . . .

Among the other more prominent types of economic regulation under the New Deal has been that administered by the Securities and Exchange Commission. This has registered the issuance of securities and exercised a certain amount of control over stock-exchange practices. It is probably a little more difficult now than before for the innocent investor or speculator to be cheated, but hardly more difficult for him to lose his money. Because there has been no real bull market since the SEC was set up, and no catastrophic break, it is a little difficult to tell what its effect would be in a setting like that of 1928 and 1929. The SEC has just begun to perform its duties of unscrambling the utility holding companies subject to reorganization under the law.

In general, the New Deal has done little, especially in this second phase, to solve the problems of our economy by planned intervention to reduce unduly high prices and to expand production and employment. Its regulatory activities have been piecemeal and peripheral, while it has waited for private enterprise to take the initiative. Yet the problems neither of agriculture nor of labor nor of government finance itself can be solved without large-scale industrial expansion.

Relief

Unemployment relief has brought the New Deal more intimately into the lives of Americans than any other of its activities. It has cost more money than anything else, although in the last two years relief appropriations have fallen below those for national defense. The administration officials in charge of relief have had wide influence on general New Deal policy.

The essential pattern of the New Deal's relief program was fixed by the old Civilian Works Administration, formed in December, 1933. Mr. Harry L. Hopkins, its head, and Mr. Aubrey Williams, his first assistant, hoped to preserve both the technical skill and the morale of the jobless by supplying them with the same sort of jobs they had had in private industry. To do this, they invented the so-called federal works projects, of which an amazing variety was devised. Federal projects eliminated the cumbersome red tape surrounding government work done under contract. They made it possible for the unemployed to be paid and supervised directly by Washington.

The CWA was followed by the FERA, then by the present WPA. The WPA was established in January, 1935. The shortcomings of the WPA have been greatly overstressed, but they are insignificant beside the gigantic fact that it has given jobs and sustenance to a minimum of 1,400,000 and a maximum of 3,300,000 persons for five years. Its work projects have added immeasurably to the national wealth; in some regions the school, health and recreation facilities it has called into existence have fairly revolutionized communal life. It must also be remembered that, as its permanent technique for dealing with the relief problem, the New Deal has been simultaneously developing its programs for unemployment insurance, old-age pensions, assistance to mothers, dependent children and the handicapped. . . .

Throughout the course of the WPA, its projects in the first instance have been chosen by local communities, and the communities have contributed in an increasing amount to the cost of materials and supervision. The most elaborate project has been the great LaGuardia airport at New York City. The WPA has built or repaired 457,000 miles of streets and roads, one-seventh of the total national mileage. It has built 23,-000 public buildings, and improved 65,-000, including schools, hospitals, jails, firehouses, athletic fields, electric-power plants. Among its many service projects perhaps the most dramatic have been its adult-education classes, through which a steady assault has been made on illiteracy. Census experts have estimated that the WPA has reduced illiteracy to less than one percent. . . .

Collective Bargaining

Soon after Mr. Roosevelt's inauguration in 1933 the New Deal's basic labor policy was established in the famous Section 7a of the NIRA. The language of this section was taken bodily from the LaGuardia-Norris labor-injunction measure of 1928. But the LaGuardia-Norris law had been essentially negative. It had simply forbidden the courts to do anything to prevent unionization. By Section 7a, the New Deal morally committed itself to intervene in the industrial struggle, to restrain open-shop employers, to make the workers' right to organize a reality. The whole law was later declared unconstitutional.

The head of the National Labor Board was Senator Wagner, who thus had the rare distinction of holding office in both legislative and executive departments. In the 1934 session of Congress, Senator Wagner first proposed a permanent, independent agency to safeguard the right of collective bargaining. Thanks largely to Mr. Wagner's deft political generalship, his bill was enacted in 1935, and the present National Labor Relations Board came into being. While the New Dealers loyally supported the Wagner bill, it was not a New Deal measure in the sense that other Roosevelt reforms have been. It is perhaps worth noting that the NLRB has never had the intimate liaison with the White House that the SEC, for example, has had.

The NLRB was greeted by a vicious, concentrated attack from industry under the leadership of the National Association of Manufacturers. A brief was published by fifty-eight Liberty League lawyers—some of the most distinguished members of the American bar—declaring the NLRB clearly unconstitutional, and inferentially inviting employers to defy it. More than one hundred injunction suits were sought in the federal courts. The NLRB was paralyzed; during the first eighteen months of its existence it was no more than a shadowy corpse. This was also the period of fierce battles in the House over the wages-and-hours bill, devised to carry out another purpose of the NRA by prohibiting competition at the expense of the workers.

It was, in addition, a period of some of the most violent disputes the country has known, culminating in the General Motors sitdown and the Memorial Day massacre of ten steel workers at Chicago. During these disturbances, the New Dealers remained largely passive. Behind-the-scenes aid was given Mr. Frank Murphy, then Michigan's Governor, in settling the automobile strike; publicly Mr. Roosevelt called for "a plague o' both your houses."

In April, 1937, the Supreme Court upheld the constitutionality of the NLRB in a five-to-four decision delivered by Mr.

Chief Justice Hughes. For the first time, the NLRB was able to discharge the duties intrusted to it. One of the most significant happenings of the last eight years has been its success in winning the confidence of the rank and file of workers. In 1938, industrial disputes fell off by one-half. A close relationship can be shown between the steady decrease in strikes for union recognition and the mounting number of complaints—now numbering about 25,000—filed with the NLRB. The workers have seemingly discovered that they can safely turn from naked economic warfare to the processes of government. The period of the NLRB's existence has witnessed enormous increases in union membership and collective bargaining. According to estimates, total union membership has risen from 3,500,000 in 1935 to about.8,000,000 at present. . . .

The net result of the New Deal's labor policy is a greater strengthening of the unions than had previously occurred in the nation's history, and this is likely to be of overwhelming importance in the future, particularly if labor becomes unified.

Agricultural Relief

The New Deal's program of agricultural relief falls into two parts. The first comprises measures to rescue the farmers who still manage to retain land ownership, by no matter how small a margin. The second includes measures for the relief of the nearly three million tenant and sharecropper families—those who have lost their access to the soil.

For the first group, the owner-operators, the New Deal has sought chiefly to reduce the burdensomeness of mortgage debt. . . .

The end of Mr. Roosevelt's second term, however, finds the New Deal's farm-mortgage policy uncertain and confused.

The other half of the New Deal's program for agricultural relief—that for tenants and sharecropers—had its start with the fierce 1934 drought. By the end of that summer, the FERA's division of Rural Rehabilitation was the sole support of 300,000 persons—the group from which came the later Okies and Arkies of California. The next year, 1935, the Resettlement Administration, headed by Under-Secretary of Agriculture Rexford G. Tugwell, was created to care for all rural relief.

This relief took multitudinous forms. The RA's chief planning zeal, however, was aimed at creating rural coöperatives and collectives, where farm families would raise their crops in fellowship. The RA inherited the PWA's Subsistence Homesteads—projects of a slightly different nature—together with coöperatives established under the FERA. These coöperatives and collectives were energetically increased. As a quite separate venture, the RA also undertook the construction of four suburban towns, intended to be models of twentieth-century planning.

After the 1936 election, and Mr. Tugwell's resignation, this part of the New Deal's rural relief program changed markedly. One reason for the shift was the bitter, uninformed criticism of sharecroppers' collectives that had arisen in the South. In 1936, 124 co-operative or collective communities were in existence; plans for many others were in preparation. The New Dealers gave assurances that this program would be abruptly halted. At the same time, the RA's name was altered to the Farm Security Administration.

To underscore its disapproval of the RA's policies, Congress—in the Bankhead Farm Tenancy Act—instructed the FSA to work toward precisely the opposite ideal, that of setting up tenants and sharecroppers as ruggedly independent farm owners. The FSA has loyally carried out this command within the limits of appropriated funds. Recently landless families were being placed on farms bought for them by FSA at the rate of about 5,000 a year. It is hoped that this rate can be perhaps doubled in the future. It is admitted, however, that only a microscopic proportion of the three million tenants and sharecroppers can be cared for in this way. The cost of farms has averaged slightly more than $5,000 apiece; tenants repay the government under a model land-tenure contract that permits larger payments in good years, smaller in bad.

The greatest part of the FSA's activity, however, has centered around its so-called rehabilitation loans. The circumstances of each tenant or sharecropper family are expertly studied; it receives a small loan—the average is about $350—for just those purposes that will most benefit it. The loan may permit the family to rent a bit of land, or to buy feed, seed or fertilizer, or to raise chickens and pigs for food, or to obtain a draft animal. More than three-quarters of a million loans have been made. This program has brought extraordinary advancement in the status of individual families. In large measure its remarkable success comes from the fact that families receiving loans are constantly advised and watched over by Department of Agriculture agents. As a separate program, the FSA has also given cash relief, for longer or shorter periods, to about 500,000 families. Back in 1933, the New

Dealers were eager to retire submarginal land—land that could never yield a decent livelihood to the communities dwelling on it. The AAA was given authority to buy and retire land with relief funds. Partly because relief appropriations have been continuously inadequate, the New Deal has made only slow progress toward this goal.

One of the most spectacular successes of the whole New Deal has been the Rural Electrification Administration, which has lent funds to local governments and private groups for the construction of electric-power lines. Allotments have now been made that will permit the building of about 240,000 miles of line, serving 700,000 farm families. In September, 1939, 135,000 miles of line were already in operation, bringing electricity to 300,000 farm homes. The REA's competition has compelled private utilities to increase their rural facilities; since it began its operations, the number of farms with electric service has jumped from about 750,000 to more than a million and a half.

Agricultural relief has been nowhere nearly adequate to rescue a stricken farm population, but it has done something, and without it conditions would have been infinitely worse.

Governmental Pioneering

If human beings still inhabit our continent two hundred years from now it is not impossible that the Roosevelt administration will be remembered chiefly for its vast engineering achievements: the Tennessee Valley Authority, Boulder Dam, Grand Coulee, Bonneville and Fort Peck. The primary purposes of these huge structures are to produce hydro-electric power in great volume at low cost, which is not only valuable in itself but offers a useful yardstick for the prices asked by private companies for the same thing, to afford flood control and irrigation, to checkmate soil erosion through proper agricultural methods, to facilitate river navigation, bring fresh supplies of water to cities and to manufacture nitrates for fertilizer. The statistical aspects of these new developments have been printed many times and need not be reviewed again in detail. The production of electric power is so enormous that it will take years to put it all effectively to work. Bonneville and Grand Coulee, for example, will furnish enough hydroelectricity to permit decentralized power-operative industry throughout the entire Northwest. Boulder Dam is not only a power generator but it includes a great aqueduct and irrigation canal. The power station is four times as great as Niagara's and two and a half times that of the big Russian plant about which the American Communists are perennially talking, the plant formerly called Dnieperstroy. The aqueduct will carry a billion gallons of water a day 240 miles over desert and through mountains to Los Angeles. The entire amount will be lifted about 1,200 feet into the air in the process. The irrigation canal removes the danger of floods from a great area in the Imperial Valley and will bring water ultimately to 1,500,000 acres.

The Tennessee Valley Authority is in some ways the most striking of all these huge enterprises. It is literally true that to a great degree it has brought a new way of life to many thousands of persons in the basin of the Tennessee River. Not only has it made cheap power abundantly available and increased its use to an almost unbelievable degree, but it has introduced new industries and made over old ones. Farmers in this area, for example, are just beginning to take advantage of a newly invented quick-freezing process for fruits and vegetables, worked out by TVA engineers in collaboration with university technicians. This improved technique means that perishable crops are perishable no longer, that the farmer is free from the problem of panic selling at whatever price the buyer cares to pay, and that his income is likely to be much augmented. Improved methods of planting, growing and harvesting crops mean greater yields and a higher standard of life, while the destruction of the soil by ruinous erosion is being stopped.

In many minds federalism is synonymous with bureaucracy if not paternalism. These dangers are being avoided in the TVA, where a striking system of decentralized federal aid has been applied. For example, when a new agricultural technique is in prospect, it is introduced county by county, neighborhood by neighborhood. A group of farmers are called together and told of the proposed idea. If they don't want it, the matter is ended for that area. If they do want it, they are likely to elect one of their own number to be the first to carry out the experiment while they watch. There is no coercion unless you call it coercion for the government to offer to help a man make more money for himself by better methods.

To Preserve Our Soil. "Soil conservation" is a dreary-sounding phrase but the subject is no more dreary than is the discussion, to any individual, of whether he is to live or die. The natural topsoil in the United States, taking the country as a whole, was nine inches deep when we began farming operations, which, for most of the continent, was only about a hundred years ago. Today the average depth of the topsoil is between five and six inches. We have lost a good third in a century; but that doesn't mean we have another two centuries to go; already 300,000,000 acres of our best land have been almost wholly destroyed. If we do not reverse this process the Middle West, the national breadbasket, will be an uninhabitable desert in a hundred years, with the empty steel and stone hulks of former skyscrapers in the cities looming above the waste as monuments to our incredible folly.

The Roosevelt administration is the first in American history to make a real effort to halt this trend. It has worked on a dozen fronts. Civilian Conservation Corps boys have built many thousands of dams and irrigation ditches. The Agricultural Adjustment Administration has for several years been paying farmers something (though the average payment is far smaller than is commonly supposed) to leave part of their land idle and to follow other methods of saving the soil. Everywhere, farmers are being taught to plow with the contours instead of running their furrows straight down the hillside. Wherever possible, good-sized areas are being turned back to the forest which for hundreds of thousands of years protected our rich American earth from such destruction as man has wrought in a decade. Insect enemies are rooted out by any one of several government agencies. All over the country people are being taught that the land should not and must not be destroyed in the space of three generations.

Mr. Roosevelt's enemies laughed at the "shelter belt" as one of his chief follies; but if they had taken the trouble to consult people who knew anything about the subject, they would have suppressed their laughter. Today the shelter belt is in existence to the extent of nearly 100,000,000 trees, and is a proved, demonstrable success. It is not, as newspaper headlines pictured it, one vast forest strip running north and south from Canada to Mexico. It is on the contrary a multitude of short strips, a mile or two long, at right angles to the direction of the prevailing winds. Eight or ten rows are set out of trees of varying height, the shortest ones being set to windward. The government and the farmer coöperate on roughly equal terms in bearing the cost of the enterprise. Today, many thousands of acres in Dust Bowl or pre-Dust Bowl conditions are being rescued to the satisfaction of everyone except the editors of Tory newspapers in big cities who doubtless haven't seen a tree for years.

To Rescue Youth. Depressions are bad enough on old people, but they are far harder on the young. Character disintegrates and morale decays when you grow up to young manhood or womanhood with no hope of getting a job, of being able to marry and raise a family. While Mr. Hoover was in the White House the depression turned loose on our highways a vagrant army of boys—and some girls—who had nowhere to go, but nowhere to stay either; who were rapidly becoming unreclaimable derelicts. The New Deal has done a heroic, unrecorded and unrecognized job in remedying many of these evils. The CCC has taken a total of about 2,000,000 young men, unemployed and without resources, and put them to work on the land, 300,000 at a time, in service that must not be less than six months or more than two years. The enrollee gets $30 a month and sends nearly all of it back to his family. The improvement in these boys, physically and mentally, is almost unbelievable unless you have seen it at first hand. What they have done for the country in the way of reforestation, soil conservation, irrigation, fire fighting and eliminating fire hazards, destruction of insect pests and aboreal diseases and road and trail building is more extensive than most people know.

The CCC is limited to 300,000, but the need that youth shall be aided is as wide as the country itself. To help fill the breach we have the National Youth Administration. One of its important activities is helping boys and girls to stay in high school or college when their family resources would make this impossible. Hundreds of thousands work ten or twenty hours a month at 30 or 40 cents an hour and this sum spells to them the difference between a education completed and an education destroyed by the economic storm. Their tasks are set and supervised by the institutions where they work, and are on the whole good and useful projects without "boondoggling." Many thousands of other young people are aided outside of school in workshops where they are given useful employment and whenever possible are taught trades and occupations in which they can subsequently earn their livelihood. No one will ever know what this work has meant to hundreds of thousands of dispirited young men and women at a time when it seemed that the whole world was against them.

White-collar Morale. Depression is no respecter of white collars. While it took away the livelihood of many millions of men who could appropriately be reëmployed at hard, outdoor work, it also destroyed the jobs of hundreds of thousands of intellectual and creative workers—scientists, teachers, musicians, painters, actors, writers and allied professions. Some stern moralists among the opponents of the New Deal philosophy were all for giving a research chemist, for example, a pick and shovel and telling him to use them or starve. Luckily this Draconian doctrine was not endorsed by those in authority who knew that the skills of its citizens are the greatest resource of a nation and that it is the worst possible policy to let them deteriorate with idleness while millions of people need the things those skills produce. Accordingly, the principle was followed of trying to put intellectuals and creative individuals to work in their own fields. WPA musicians have given an incredible number of concerts to an astronomical number of people and have taught music to thousands of aspirants who could not afford to pay for private instruction. The artistic renaissance brought about by the painting and sculpture projects is a story by itself which space does not permit us to tell here. The Writers' Project has produced a large number of books good enough so that private publishers, operating through the normal channels of trade, have been glad to put these volumes on their lists. Notable is the American Guide Series which has done for the individual states a long needed job of research and reporting.

The Federal Theatre Project was perhaps the best known of these enterprises. It put on the boards many plays of an experimental or special character which commercial producers would not touch but to which vast numbers of people were glad to go and to pay for their seats. In some of its techniques and notably the

"Living Newspaper" it has left a permanent impression upon the American theatre. It was finally killed not because of any demerits but by a hill-billy mentality in Congress actuated chiefly by the backwoods notion that "all play actin' is wicked."

In many ways the Roosevelt administration has fostered recreation in this country. WPA workers and those from other relief agencies have built municipal golf and tennis courts, playgrounds, swimming pools, picnic areas in parks throughout the country. People have been taught to sing or to play musical instruments. Federal theatre companies have presented dramas to hundreds of thousands of people of whom it is literally true that they had never seen a dramatic presentation before. Even the night schools for adults through which have passed staggering numbers of persons come under the heading of recreation as well as self-advancement.

Social Security. In nothing has the change in our thinking in eight years been so extraordinary as in relation to aiding those who are victims of the economic storm, either through unemployment at any age or through arriving in the sunset years of life without sufficient means. In 1932 the obligation of the state to assist its citizens under these circumstances was admitted in practically every other civilized country in the world; but the people of the United States were still dominated sufficiently by an outmoded frontier psychology so that many of them, perhaps a majority, insisted that if you lose a job, or grow old without savings, it is your own fault and you must take the consequences even though those consequences include going to the ragged edge of starvation. Today

the government in coöperation with the states gives aid at least during the first few weeks to every unemployed person in the occupations that are covered (the important exceptions are domestic work and agricultural labor). The benefits vary from state to state, but in general, the unemployed man gets about 50 percent of his regular pay, up to $15 a week based on pay of $30, for a maximum of three or four months. The unemployment-insurance offices also make every effort to help him find a job, having taken over all other government agencies that existed for the same purpose....

The federal government is also helping blind persons and dependent children who are not otherwise cared for in the foregoing plan. It contributes a maximum of $20 a month, matching an equal contribution from the state. Including dependent children, and the helpless aged, about 2,600,000 persons are being assisted this year.

Housing and Home Financing. Nobody needs to be told today that millions of Americans live in substandard houses. Most of the bad slums are in the cities, but not all. The Roosevelt administration has been the first to make any real attempt to ameliorate these conditions. First through the Public Works Administration and later through the United States Housing Authority, some of the worst slums in the United States have been destroyed and their inhabitants, or an equivalent number of the very poor, have been moved into new buildings which in comparison are palaces and are literally, in regard to light and air and open space, far better than the dwellings for which wealthy people on New York's Park Avenue pay $20,000 or $30,000 a year in rent.

The USHA has loaned to the communities about $600,000,000, which is going into very nearly the safest investment in the world. (In view of the fact that this money is loaned and not given away, the failure of Congress to utilize double or treble or ten times this amount can only be due to political pressure by the private real-estate interests who benefit financially when there is a shortage of housing and who often make their biggest profits on overcrowded, filthy and disease-breeding slums.) This money will be used, by the local communities who get it, to construct about 134,000 dwelling units in which half a million people will live. Already, 179 projects are under construction in 24 states, the District of Columbia, Hawaii and Puerto Rico. People are already living in twelve of these projects. The average rental is about $14 per month per unit, ranging from a low figure of $6.59 in the South to $16.64 in New York City. A small additional fee is charged for water, gas, electricity and heat. As a rule, family income cannot be more than five times the rent. The government and states together make annual contributions to bridge the gap between what the families can afford to pay in rent and the actual cost of operation and amortization of the investment. The municipality must pay at least 20 percent of this amount and the government's contribution is limited by law to 3.25 percent of the total cost.

The government has also done a great deal to aid in solving the housing problem for other elements in the community than the extremely poor. The Federal Housing Administration, which is now about five years old, assists in financing the building of new homes and the modernization and repair of old ones. It does so not by lending government money outright, but by guaranteeing loans made on mortgage by banks and other lending institutions. The total amount of business it has underwritten amounts to the impressive sum of more than $4,-600,000,000. Of this, about $2,000,000,-000 represents the building of new houses for single families. One-half of these families have incomes of $2,500 or less; they pay five percent down and the balance over as long as fifteen years. The maximum interest rate is 4.5 percent, which, while it seems to many disinterested observers to be far higher than necessary, is nevertheless the lowest the country has ever seen. When the FHA was established, the total number of of houses built in the country had sunk to the extremely low level of 50,000 a year. It has now risen to about 460,000 annually, one-half of which are built with government guarantee. Forty percent of these houses are built in small towns where mortgage money has always been notoriously scarce.

The FHA has also guaranteed loans for modernization and improvement amounting to about $1,000,000,000. It has aided builders of group housing or houses for rental to a value of $113,000,-000 to care for 30,000 families. Business plants have been repaired or modernized to a number of 300,000 and the total number of houses involved in operations of various types is about 2,000,000.

When Mr. Roosevelt came into office, millions of city dwellers and farmers alike were on the point of losing their homes because of mortgage foreclosure, and it was believed urgently necessary to stop this process. This has been done through such instrumentalities as the Home Owners' Loan Corporation and the Farm Credit Administration.

The Home Owners' Loan Corporation

has helped about one million distressed owners of homes. The total bonds it has been authorized to issue amounted to nearly $5,000,000,000, of which about $2,700,000,000 are outstanding. Twenty-three percent of the total indebtedness has been paid off and a great part of the remainder is in process of liquidation, in spite of the fact that the HOLC was ordered to lend money to people who couldn't get it anywhere else. The average loan is $3,000 and the interest rate has been cut from 5 to 4.5 percent. The length of time for repayment has been extended by Congress from fifteen to twenty-five years. The HOLC is in process of liquidation, the number of employees having been cut from 22,000 to 11,000. . . .

Looking Backward

. . . One need only recall what conditions were in 1932 to realize the amazing change in our national thinking that has taken place in eight years. While there is still complaint about paternalism and centralized government (from the Republicans who were the great exponents of these ideas, applied under special circumstances, for the first seventy-five years of their party's life) it is obvious that even the critics are only halfhearted in what they say.

As a nation we have agreed, once and forever, that the individual must not bear the sole responsibility for his failure to cope with economic problems of unemployment or old age which are, quite obviously, beyond his powers, and that society as a whole must take over a substantial part of the burden.

We have at last learned that laissez-faire has been dead for years; that the unguided lust of the business man for profit does not infallibly produce Utopia.

And finally, we have reaffirmed in these past eight years an early American doctrine that had been all but forgotten in preceding decades: that the country exists for the welfare and happiness of all its inhabitants; and that when this condition is not met, reformation is in order no matter how drastic it may be or how much it may be disliked by existing privileged minorities.

What It All Means

The New Deal, even in its second term, has clearly done far more for the general welfare of the country and its citizens than any administration in the previous history of the nation. Its relief for underprivileged producers in city and country, though inadequate to the need, has been indispensable. Without this relief an appalling amount of misery would have resulted, and a dangerous political upheaval might have occurred. Since the expenditure of money for relief—even the insufficient amounts recently appropriated—has been the principal target of the administration's conservative enemies, this accomplishment alone would be sufficient reason for support of the New Deal. The assertion of the reactionaries that if the federal budget were balanced by cutting expenses, business would revive sharply enough to absorb the unemployed and make relief expenditures unnecessary, is incapable of proof and seems highly improbable.

In addition, the New Deal in this second period has accomplished much of permanent benefit to the nation. Perhaps its most important achievement was the National Labor Relations Act, the result of which was to inhibit employers' opposition to union organization and true collective bargaining, so that trade-union membership was more than doubled. This was not a mere act of justice; it was the laying of a solid foundation for our society in the future. Without a strong, alert and independent labor movement a modern industrial nation is in constant danger from the enemies of political and social democracy. Second only to the strengthening of unions is the establishment of minimum labor standards. The fury with which reactionaries have attacked these two labor measures is an index of their importance.

Other permanent improvements are the impetus given to conservation of soil and forests, the many-sided TVA, a great road-building program, flood control, a good beginning at slum clearance and adequate housing for those not provided for by private construction, great hydroelectric projects, extension of electricity at reasonable rates through the Rural Electrification Administration, and the inauguration of insurance against unemployment and the other forms of social security.

The government as an instrument of democratic action in the future has also been strengthened and renovated. This is not merely a matter of the addition of many new agencies, but of the more efficient organization of the whole executive department—including a planning board under the President which so far has been relatively unimportant but is capable of future development. The Courts, too, have been revivified, partly by legislation, but principally by excellent new appointments, so that we now have a Supreme Court which is abreast of the times.

It is improbable that these permanent changes will be or even can be destroyed by any new administration.

All these extraordinary accomplishments must be remembered when we speak of the points at which the New Deal has been disappointing in its second phase. The most important of these is of course its failure to discover or apply a genuine remedy for the stagnation of our economy, and for unemployment. These years have seen no return to the conditions of 1932 or 1933, to be sure, but on the other hand no great or permanent improvement in national income, production or employment above the level already achieved in 1936. Nor have they seen the adoption of any important new means of bringing about such improvement. The President has apparently been hoping continually that business and investment would gain momentum of their own accord, while business spokesmen have been blaming what they called the hostile attitude of the New Deal for a lack of confidence which they charged with responsibility for retarding advance. It is doubtful, however, whether they are right about this, in the view of economists who have studied the problem intensively.

On two occasions during the past few years the President has heeded business advice, at least in part, by trying to cut recovery expenditures in the hope that a permanent improvement in business was in prospect—once in 1937 and again in 1939. On both occasions a sharp slump followed. The upswing which was occurring when the cuts were made turned out to have been due to an accumulation of inventories by business, which overshot the demand from consumers, and reaction under such circumstances was inevitable.

The reason for the failure of our economy to come back to really prosperous levels is not known with certainty, but there is no such mystery about it as many believe. Economists of varying schools have pointed out several causes, each of which undoubtedly plays a part. The question concerns how large a part each plays, but we do not need to wait for the answer to that question in order to devise and apply remedial action.

One assigned reason is the failure of construction fully to revive. Closely associated with this is the high price of steel, other capital goods, and high building costs themselves. Such progress as has been made is largely due to government efforts to reduce the price of and access to capital for home-owners through the FHA, and the valuable but insufficient work of the USHA in organizing and financing large low-cost housing projects. The anti-trust prosecutions of the Department of Justice may help in the future.

Another assigned reason is high prices of industrial products in general. Too few privately controlled industries follow the policy of low prices leading to enlarged sales. Anti-trust action may remedy this in the relatively few cases in which illegal monopoly exists, but that is hardly enough.

The third important reason is the lack of old or rapidly expanding new industries in which capital investment may take place. The government might remedy this situation by a drastic railroad-reorganization program, or by a carefully planned scheme of large-scale public investment. It has not moved in either direction.

The President's failure to make more progress in tackling the central problem of our economy is probably due mainly to two things—the strengthening of conservative opposition, especially since the 1938 election, and concentration on the European situation. The country is weaker, whether for war or for peace, because of this slackening of pace in the New Deal. If our foreign policy can avoid involvement in the war, we shall be fortunate. But in any case we should not rely on war, whether we are in it or not, to do for us the domestic job that remains. If the New Deal is to deserve our support in the future, it must not rest on what it has already done, great as that is, but tell us how it is going to finish the task.

REXFORD G. TUGWELL (1891–) played in the
later New Deal something of the role that Raymond
Moley did in its early days. A professor of economics at
Columbia, Tugwell served FDR as undersecretary of
agriculture and as a general idea man. Moley left the
New Deal disillusioned and concerned, but Tugwell in
retrospect sees it as a rich, successful, and distinctively
American experiment in democratic reform. The
difference in the reaction of the two men is a good
measure of the degree of change that took place within
the New Deal itself.*

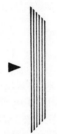

The New Deal in Retrospect

I

It may seem strange—incongruous—to
speak of President Roosevelt as in direct
descent, politically, from Ignatius Donnelley [sic], Pitchfork Ben Tillman, Tom
Watson, Sockless Jerry Simpson and
Mary Elizabeth Lease, that wild-eyed
agrarian female radical who shouted up
and down American in 1890 that farmers
ought to raise less corn and more hell.
It is nevertheless true that President
Roosevelt owed his election largely—not,
of course, wholly—to the movement, long
gathering force, long frustrated, which
was headed by Donnelley and others of
the Farmers' Alliance, the Grangers, and
the Populists in the Midwest and the
South of the last century. It would be
more accurate to say that President
Roosevelt was in direct descent from
Bryan, and that Bryan had been the in-
heritor of all the agrarian unrest. That
he won, as Bryan could not, was because
the depression of 1929 was worse than
that of 1893, and because the number of
those who were shaken in their Republicanism was greater in proportion to the
whole. . . .

On the whole, with minor setbacks,
the increase in productivity in America,
together with the exploitation of a continent still largely unexhausted by soil
erosion and the depletion of other resources, had kept the challenging critics
of things-as-they-are from becoming a
majority until 1932. The situation which

* Rexford G. Tugwell, "The New Deal in Retrospect," *Western Political Quarterly*,
vol. 1, no. 1, (December 1948), pp. 373–385.

existed after World War I was one in which complacency, conservatism, loyal mutual support between government and business, together with isolation, seemed to a majority of the electorate to be a sufficient policy for the times. People wanted normalcy after their adventure abroad. Mr. Hoover, however, inheriting what had now become a tradition fixed by Harding and Coolidge, found himself unable to overcome a fast-developing crisis in economic life which began in the late '20's. And he was, of course, humiliatingly defeated by President Roosevelt in 1932, after serving for one term. He had won, it will be remembered, from Smith in 1928. But that campaign had been less dramatic than the concurrent phenomena of the bull market. The economic issue was not yet ready for political exploitation. There was still prosperity for almost everyone but the farmers.

What was the economic crisis? And how far had it gone by 1932? It had begun—and here is the connection with the agrarians and the long western disaffection which had been so brilliantly personified by Bryan—by a disastrous fall of farm prices in 1920-21. There had begun, then, one of those unbalanced deflationary movements which so often have occurred in American economic life as a result of the unplanned and uncontrolled actions of economic groups in pursuit of private interests. The world had wanted farm products in great quantity during the war; after it was over, an expanded agriculture found its markets failing and its prices going down. But prices of manufactured goods (which the farmer must buy) stayed high. It took more unprocessed wheat, hogs, cotton, or corn to buy farm machinery, or even processed food and fibre, than ever

before. Presently it took almost twice as much, and farmers felt that not only natural causes were at fault. They were certain that the deflation was the result of policies originated in Washington by those who were unfriendly. . . .

The farm price decline had begun in 1920. City people—industrialists, bankers, and even workers—are not much inclined to be concerned with farmers' woes—at least they had not been in the '20's. And otherwhere than in agriculture a great boom had been going on. It had been a peculiarity of this boom that prices had not gone up. In fact, nonfarm commodity prices had been remarkably stable from 1920 to 1928. The publicity men of the industrialists had exploited this fact by talking about "profitless prosperity." But, of course, it had not actually been profitless. What had been happening as a result of the many technical advances during the war could now be understood; efficiency was greater and costs were coming down. Profits, in spite of stable prices, were going up and up.

It is one of the unalterable conditions for the successful continuation of large-scale industry that purchasing power among consumers must be sufficient to carry off the volume produced. In order to maintain purchasing power in volume, consumers' incomes and the total of prices attached to goods and services for sale must be roughly equal. They cannot be equal unless prices come down as costs come down; otherwise, the increasing profits go into more factories and increased production. In the long run warehouses fill with goods for which there is no demand. This is a very short and, because short, inaccurate account of the basic trouble in 1929. It leaves out, for instance, the effect of the vast pools of sterile savings, and also those which financed the wild speculation after 1927. But it does emphasize the fact that, by 1929, productive power *had* far outrun purchasing power. The farmers had first been priced out of the market; then other consumers had followed; and all the time vast increases in plant were being made. Also vast speculations were taking place with the ever-growing surpluses of business. Suddenly it was seen that the huge debts contracted at the inflated levels of speculation could not be paid. All creditors tried to force payment of debts to them at once. There was panic.

II

The Republican answer to the spreading depression after 1928 had been, first to deny its seriousness, and then to encourage the raising of private relief funds. Mr. Hoover was reluctant to admit that the government had any responsibility at all. But he did consent to the setting up of the Reconstruction Finance Corporation for business relief, and this was one phase of the famous "trickle" theory which was afterward emphasized by the Democrats. The R.F.C. was finally authorized, also, to loan $300,-000,000 to the states for relief; and a farm aid program, which offered more succor for processors than for farmers, was begun. But that was Mr. Hoover's limit. He would not admit, any more than Coolidge had, that the federal government had a direct responsibility to the people for their welfare.

The campaign of 1932 came after almost four years of grinding deflation, succeeding almost a decade of agricultural depression. There were idle factories, unemployment, hunger—all the phenomena of industrial paralysis. During this time, Mr. Roosevelt was governor of New York where the miseries of depression were felt to their utmost. Toward the end of Mr. Hoover's administration it became quite obvious that the time was coming for a new man and a new program; he had lost practically all his popular support. What could be more logical than that the Governor of the Empire State, a life-long liberal, an experienced and popular public figure, should succeed to the Presidency.

It was one of those times, which come occasionally in the life of the nation, when the nomination for the Presidency is especially valuable, because, unless mistakes are made, winning is a foregone conclusion. Mr. Roosevelt was a professional politician. He was well aware of the possibilities. There had been, in fact, two most astute agents at work for years —Louis McHenry Howe and James A. Farley—rounding up delegates: or rather, preparing to round up when the time should arrive. There was opposition to be expected. The conservative wing of the party had the choice of Byrd of Virginia and Ritchie of Maryland; and Smith naturally felt himself entitled to another chance since he had sacrificed himself in 1928. Developing events, however, favored President Roosevelt rather than an outright conservative. The depression deepened. Disillusionment with Republicanism extended itself to the normally Republican middle classes; and the Republican farmers were awaiting the word of hope to abandon their political leaders if not their party.

There was drama in the nomination of 1932 in Chicago. Not until President Roosevelt's own forces had worked out a modus operandi with a substantial section of the Southern Democracy could the business be concluded. In this it was arranged for Mr. Garner of Texas to be Vice-President. This, it might be said, added to the fact that some seventeen chairmanships of committees in the new Congress were to be held by Southerners, would present President Roosevelt with a sectional problem which would torment him throughout his more than twelve years in the Presidency. For the West, the South, and the big city machines would make a difficult team to handle. And often compromises and trades would be necessary which would emasculate what it was proposed to do. Nevertheless, it was a condition of nomination that such a compromise should take place. And President Roosevelt, an Easterner, did join the South and the West more successfully than any politician had been able to do since the Civil War. This was where his happiest faculties had their fullest scope.

The election was less dramatic. The campaign, because its outcome became so favorable in prospect, turned into a cautious statement of progressive hopes and beliefs, the items of which had been familiar since the times of Bryan, T. R. Roosevelt, and Wilson. Nevertheless, it was a statement, however tame, of progressive intentions. Perhaps the fact that a *progressive* was to succeed Hoover, after Harding and Coolidge, intensified the fears of Wall Street. When a *Roosevelt* administration became a certainty, it became equally certain that new forces would come into control. Perhaps this may have caused the deflation to run deeper than it otherwise might. Everyone was trying to become liquid—free of debt—at once. And everyone distrusted the shaky institutions of finance, which were suspected of having made vast loans abroad and to industrialists at home, with depositors' funds, which would

never be repaid. The struggles to collect, and the unwillingness of depositors to trust them further, brought President Roosevelt to his inauguration day in the midst of complete economic paralysis, with banks closing, Governors declaring bank holidays—that is, moratoria—unemployment at twelve or thirteen millions, hardship and misery everywhere. The great new post-war factories were now closed, transportation systems were bankrupt and idle. Only soup kitchens and what were called "Hoovervilles"—shack villages on dump heaps—were busy.

To a nation thus paralyzed and sunk in despair, a golden voice proclaimed in the First Inaugural that Americans had nothing to fear but fear itself. It seemed as though a great sleeper awoke at that call and found that, after all, he had a useful strength. He stretched and looked for ways to use it. No less than 460,000 citizens wrote personally to their President as a result of this one speech. It swamped the White House facilities, but it showed what a welcome change Roosevelt was after Hoover. The people had a man.

The first measures had to be emergency ones: to assuage fears, to relieve suffering, and to set up more equal exchange among those who made various kinds of goods and provided various kinds of services. Measures looking to longer-run social security could await a measure of recovery. So, in fact, could the reforms still holding over, remaining to be done, from older progressive regimes—notably the Wilsonian, though some of that program had been achieved then.

Theoretically the Wilsonian measures should have prevented what had happened in 1929 and subsequently. And Democrats really had the choice of saying that their reforms had been sabotaged by Republican administrations or admitting frankly what they had done had not been enough. In the Roosevelt campaign the candidate practically admitted the deficiency by way of redefining progressivism. He called it the New Deal.

The A.A.A. was devised to restore agriculture to "parity" in the national community and bring farmers again into the concert of economic interests. And the N.R.A. was provided to encourage the immediate resumption of industrial activity—the President's re-employment agreement, of which the well-remembered symbol was the Blue Eagle. And along with this, the financial system was bolstered by emergency loans to banks by the R.F.C. which amounted to a guarantee of deposits, gold was made a government monopoly, and the dollar devalued so that debts could be paid in cheaper money. This was inflation. In an instant, people's savings, insurance policies, bank deposits, etc., lost about one-third of their value. But hardly anyone even noticed this; they were worth very little anyway in a national debacle....

III

The administration of the new measures was necessarily ragged. For relief, for instance, there was no organization at all and one had to be devised offhand by Hopkins and his helpers—Williams, Gill, Hunter, Baker and others—and long chances had to be taken "in getting the money out." The same was true of the A.A.A. Scores of thousands of employees had to be engaged and trained on the job to do things which were just the reverse of all accepted bureaucratic rules and practices. And as for the N.R.A.— under General Johnson its administra-

tion immediately became a caricature of decent procedure.

Impromptu organization and freehand administration brought criticism even from those who were benefiting most; the sharpest dissent came from the business community, which was smarting from its own failure and from the humiliating need to be bailed out and set on its feet again. During the subsequent period, when it came to putting through certain reforms, business, again fairly prosperous, was about as vigorous in its opposition as though it had not been prostrate a year or two before. Nevertheless, a Securities and Exchange Act was passed and the Anti-Trust Division of the Department of Justice was given new life under Mr. Thurman Arnold. These will be recognized as theretofore unfinished business on the progressive agenda.

It can be imagined, even by those who belong to a generation which has no recollection of the incidents of those years, what life was like in the United States during the Great Depression following 1929 and also during the years of recovery, beginning in 1933. The years between the crash and the Roosevelt inauguration, when the nation was finally told that recovery was not hopeless but waited only for effort of the people themselves, were drab and miserable. There was shame, lost pride and broken initiative as well as hunger, cold and sickness. Perhaps the deflation had run its course by March of '33. It was said afterward by the President's enemies that this was so and that his measures had rather retarded than assisted. But no one thought so then. His voice came to them over the radio in the cultivated accents of Groton and Harvard; but it was warm and reassuring. What he said to do was done, even by the Congress. For the moment the Southern reactionaries were willing to give their support; and the business community which might have objected was hopelessly discredited.

IV

There will always be question, I suppose, whether, when the policies of reaction were bankrupt and even the most pushing private interests were frightened for once into considering the state of the nation, more might not have been done. For the genuinely constructive part of the New Deal would consist, not in relieving the miseries and anxieties of depression, and not even in reforms which had been long delayed, but in taking at least the minimum measures to insure that depression might not recur. It is often said, for instance—and as often denied—that in that spring of 1933 a genuine national banking, credit, and currency-issuing system might have been set up. The sanctity of banking and bankers of the old sort had certainly evaporated. Merely to belong to a profession which had taken people's funds for safekeeping and failed to keep them safe at all was to be under suspicion. And to this there were added the doubtful investment of depositors' funds, and speculations in the money market and in brokers' loans, to say nothing of proved participation in the orgiastic bull-market itself. And perhaps the public in general was the more severe for feeling guilty itself. For participation in stock gambling had been incredibly widespread. Perhaps no one would have objected much to any suggestion for change which would have made such activities impossible in the future. And the Federal Reserve System—which had itself been devised in the liberal times of Wilson,

although those who had studied its history knew it to be a compromise—had utterly failed to do what its authors and defenders had claimed for it: control speculation, prevent misuse of funds, and decentralize the money power. It seemed rather to have contributed to than to have checked the fatal succession of events which had led to the crash.

Mr. Laski, a shrewd observer of the American scene, in his *The American Presidency,* says flatly that President Roosevelt went as far as he could have gone, and he mentions specifically the criticism that the situation in 1933 was not seized on to nationalize the financial system. People who hold such views, he says, do not understand the American system. A President cannot seize occasions to establish institutions which outrun people's understanding of what is appropriate. He must wait for opinion to precede any such action.

The answer might be made to this, that opinion was ready enough, but that President Roosevelt was not—that there was no one who knew how to set up a better system, and, especially, no one available to President Roosevelt. As a matter of fact, Wall Street—people like Thomas Lamont, Russel Leffingwell, Walter W. Stewart, and others—had, together with such orthodox university authorities as H. Parker Willis, B. M. Anderson, E. W. Kemmerer, et al., a monopoly of knowledge and competence in the field of money and banking. And they, all of them, had vested interests in the Federal Reserve System. There was no one in the United States, like Keynes in Britain, who represented a genuinely alternative opinion and who could have carried out a reform.

At any rate, what President Roosevelt chose to do was to take such measures as would relieve stress—segregation of gold, devaluation of the dollar, reopening of the banks with reassurance to depositors, extension of more liberal credits to farmers and home owners, expansion of loans to banks and other businesses by the already existing R.F.C. All these were intended to renew confidence in old institutions as an alternative to creating new ones.

As to Mr. Laski's dictum that American Presidents may not get ahead of established opinion, it may be ventured that the great ones among them always have—which is one characteristic of their greatness. Jefferson made the Louisiana purchase, Monroe issued a famous hands-off warning to other powers, Lincoln appointed Grant and freed the slaves, Theodore Roosevelt created a Panama to contain the Canal, Wilson committed us to the League of Nations (it was only an error in method which prevented ratification), and President Roosevelt himself certainly took chances of the same sort, some successful, some not. Passamaquoddy, the Florida ship canal, and the subsistence homestead programs were not successes; nor was the N.R.A. But the T.V.A., the Civilian Conservation Corps, the A.A.A. and several others, were. It is too much to say that our President cannot assume a position of leadership. That there are limits no one would deny. The real question here is whether President Roosevelt did not miss a great opportunity which a Wilson, for instance, would have exploited to the limit....

V

What is involved here is the Roosevelt method. He did seek not only relief from the crisis of those years, but the means of preventing new ones. He chose to do it, however, by political finesse rather than by coups of the sort by which Jefferson took Louisiana or even by the bolder kind of leadership which he showed later with respect to the coming war. He preferred to manipulate interests against one another until the weight was on the side he wanted it to be on and was sufficient for the purpose. In this, his method is reminiscent of that of Lincoln, who also was a great improviser and knew the uses of compromise. He encouraged this group, discouraged or ignored that one, meted out discreet punishment, gave rewards—and, because he had a long time in which to do it, came out with something. It was not usually something new and neatly shaped to its purpose; but rather something misshaped by compromise and reluctant agreement, awkward, hard to operate, completely satisfactory to no one. But it did get a measure of the necessary result.

He utilized the potential strength of the farm lobby and its Congressional bloc, together with the temporary weakness of the industrial lobbies and their representatives, to establish agriculture in a new and very much improved bargaining position. It is true that, in administration, it would turn out to be about as favorable to the processors of farm products, to financial institutions dependent on agriculture and to the vast bureaucracy of the Farm Bureau and the state colleges as to the farmers themselves, and that it would pretty much exclude from its benefits sharecroppers and farm labor. But it was, undoubtedly, something. And it would probably offer enormous resistance to any such deflation as had happened in 1920-21.

A similar attempt to establish good businesses in a strong competitive position in the economy vis-a-vis those which were not good—that is, businesses which would be fair to labor, would bargain collectively, and would adhere to fair standards of competition against those which would not—completely broke down from maladministration amid the wholesale welter of sharp practice, selfishness and greed which characterized the N.R.A. in its later stages. But by then business was on its feet anyway; and business, good or bad, was not likely to suffer generally in the American economy.

Aside from this, a succession of laws, and continuing favoritism in their administration, established labor in such a bargaining position as it had never occupied before. It is sometimes said that the New Deal ended in 1936 with the Wagner-Steagall Housing Act; but the consolidation of labor's position as a favored claimant for a share in the national income continued at least until 1938, when the Fair Labor Standards Act was passed. This more or less completed a system, rather incoherent and rickety, which had begun with the 7A clauses in the N.R.A. Act, the labor provisions, and had continued through the National Labor Relations Act in 1935.

Certain other measures provided limits to future deflations. After the Social Security System was set up, however awkward and insufficient it may have been, the kind of ultimate, squalid misery which had been so prevalent from 1929 to 1933 would not be possible again so long as we had any national income to distribute. There was nothing bold about this and other similar measures; they had been commonplace in Germany, the United Kingdom and elsewhere for two generations; but American businessmen seemed to think—or at least said—that they led straight to Communism. And they required characteristic Roosevelt maneuvering to achieve.

What could save and justify the Roosevelt New Deal was not, however, its minima, its bulwarks against renewed deflations and unbalance. These were

good for what they were. But what was needed much more was an increase in the national income through renewed and intensified production. President Roosevelt had to cure a paralysis of the social organism brought about by the coiling constrictions of a *laissez faire* in the last stages of its logical development from individual enterprise to price-controlling and production-reducing monopoly. One way to attack this was through government spending, which was desirable for other reasons as well—relief of poverty, the building up of resources such as water power and reclamation projects, and the rehabilitation of farms, neglected forests and parks, and blighted urban areas. The difficulty with this was that it had to precede the collection of taxes on the income it might generate, and that an annual and balanced budget was a fetish which had survived even the depression. People with savings and insurance and people on salary knew well enough what happend when the budget was unbalanced. It made their dollars less valuable. And they were against it, along with the larger financiers. President Roosevelt always had trouble with this. And he was always reluctant to do as much as was necessary to get the result of a productivity which would have buried the investment in spending in an avalanche of goods. Not until he learned to trust Keynes did he understand what had to be done, in realistic magnitudes, if the result was to be got in that way. Perhaps he did not actually learn it until the magnificent outpouring of goods for war began after the New Deal days were over....

VI

To the backward look, President Roosevelt and his New Deal have a pattern and a meaning which, in the midst of the maneuverings and compromises of the time, was often lost sight of—by everyone but President Roosevelt himself. Inconsistency did not bother him greatly, provided there was an advantage —even if only a slight one—for the policy he wanted. It did not worry him overmuch to live in turmoil. And the constant attacks to which he was subjected by the press, even if unpleasant, were rather favorable than otherwise for what he expected to accomplish. It did not decrease the confidence common folk had in him to have constantly on view the hatred borne their champion by those whom they mistrusted.

There were few who ever saw him with the mask of confidence removed. The gaiety of his laughter in time of fear echoed not only through the unaccustomed rooms of the White House, but symbolically in every home in the land. And if he was often uncertain, that was, as he said, because he was the quarterback of a team which had to be directed on the field, and it was not a fundamental uncertainty, only a tentativeness about tactic. There was necessarily improvisation, because there had been no planning. There would be failures. But the team would ultimately win. Its members might seem ill-assorted. They might be zealous to carry the ball over often; and they might even indulge in some sabotage, if they thought they could get away with it, in favor of friends or in their own political interest. But he was the captain as well as the quarterback. It was his game; and on the whole it was his victory. Looking back from the fourth year of life in America since his death, men know how much poorer they are without him. Perhaps one test of the New Deal's worth was the great grief of common folk everywhere when the news of his death came to them so suddenly in

April of 1945. They knew, even if more analytical critics did not, that they had lost a champion, even a friend. Their judgment must always temper that of objective historians.

The New Deal may have been a progressive interlude in an America predominantly reactionary. That still remains to be seen. The personality of Roosevelt, like that of Lincoln, who, in spite of superficial difference, he so much resembles, confuses the judgment. His maneuverings, his continual trading of what he thought were small advantages for what he thought were large ones, his ability to make the most incongruous assistants work together as a team, the fact that he had a scheme in mind (as can be seen by rereading the Campaign Speeches of 1932), and that he saw most of it carried out—all this must be taken into account. He spent all his days in office work not only, as during the war, for his nation's survival, but for the strengthening in it of those groups and forces which he judged to be needful, creative, democratic, tolerant and kindly. Whether and to what extent he succeeded will become clear as time passes. It seems to me that we have gained some parity or balance among economic groups, that we approach clearer designs of what we must do, and that we have clearly established the minima of social security—and this was what Roosevelt meant by "New Deal." The critical judgment as to all these matters and as to others will no doubt become sharper and more rational; but those who have the advantage of distance and reflection will not have the memorial treasure of his presence. That, to those who knew him, will always be among the most precious of their possessions and the most illuminating of their guides.

CHARLES A. BEARD (1874–1948) has had, with Frederick Jackson Turner, the greatest influence on American historical writing in the twentieth century. Beginning with his *Economic Interpretation of the Constitution* in 1912, Beard for decades interpreted the American past and present with special reference to the controlling power of economic organization. Originally committed to reform, he was too uncertain of human performance to trust to reformers, and above all he feared the corrupting influence of war. In collaboration with the lawyer and political scientist GEORGE H. E. SMITH (1898–1962) he reviewed the work of the New Deal, with a viewpoint strongly affected by the imminence of American involvement in World War II. His last major works were scathing critiques of FDR's prewar and wartime diplomacy.*

An Epitome of Characteristics

... Without laying any claims whatever to an ability to reduce the New Deal to an exact science, we offer the following statement about it as summing up in brief form the primary characteristics of the dispensation which bears this name.

1. The problems presented to the New Deal in 1933, the ideas adopted by it, and the interests expressed in it had long been phases of American history. The New Deal continued and accentuated certain ideas and interests and was thus a prolongation of history, not a break with history.

2. In 1933, a large number of property owners, or claimants, in the United States—farmers, urban dwellers, manufacturers, and investors—were in economic distress and were unwilling to accept the drastic liquidation which alone, according to the creed they professed to live by, could permit, on a "sound" basis, the revival of business activities called "prosperity." They had rejected general liquidation in 1932 when the Reconstruction Finance Corporation was created under President Hoover to put government credit under banks, railways, and other institutions in distress, and they rejected it more emphatically in 1933.

3. The New Deal continued and extended the policy of substituting government inflation, risk, experiment, and,

indeed, speculation, for almost complete private responsibility in this respect; and this substitution was initiated and progressively developed at the request, or with the connivance, of powerful leaders in banking, industry, agriculture, and labor organizations; the full consequences of this policy, along with a number of social reforms, constitute the sum and substance of the New Deal in domestic affairs.

4. What would have happened if the Federal Government had not yielded to the demands of bankers, insurance company presidents, directors of railways, heads of lending institutions, and other leaders in finance in 1932 and 1933, if it had refused to place the whole public credit of the United States under private business and private property in distress, is not and cannot be known. A refusal on the part of the Government might have been more disastrous for the country, for business and property, than the most hotly condemned features of the New Deal as it appeared in 1940.

5. The New Deal was no revolution in class arrangements, no proletarian upheaval, no fabrication designed by socialists. It sprang essentially from the efforts of propertied classes in distress to save their claims to farms, homes, banks, railways, financial institutions, and investments from thoroughgoing liquidation in the direction of actual values, by forcing the Government of the United States to underwrite their nominal claims to values with money or credit borrowed at the risk of coming generations.

6. After the New Deal was well under way, after government underwriting had failed to restore property values and prosperity, wide-spread acceptance was found for the idea that government spending is a motive force absolutely necessary to keeping the productive economy running at even a moderate tempo; and in 1940 nearly all discretion and criticism in this respect were abandoned under the justification of national defense, perhaps on the hypothesis that enormous deficits for armaments are financially less dangerous than smaller deficits for housing, schools, and public works.

7. While public credit was being placed under shaken financial structures in private hands and currency was being released from the banking wreckage, all the primary private controls over banking, currency, and public borrowing—controls which had limited government spending, borrowing, and currency manipulation in times past—were transferred from private hands to a sovereign government in Washington; and, as an additional price politically necessary, borrowing and spending were also directed to the relief of propertyless persons, on a huge scale.

8. In creating a large number of federal financial agencies charged with underwriting distressed private interests, Congress transferred the primary controls over public credit to the Chief Executive, to be exercised by him through subordinates of his own choosing, and vested in him and his agents large discretionary powers in committing the Treasury to loans, refunding schemes, property management, and other financial obligations. In this respect Congress said, in effect, "All power to the President," at least "for the emergency," which never grew less.

9. Through credit operations, designed to prevent a "natural" liquidation of interests suffering from economic misfortunes, federal finance penetrated nearly every phase of private finance and

credit, and state and local finance. It thus entangled the Federal Government in the vicissitudes of private transactions and economic activities and in the vicissitudes of public transactions and activities in states, cities, counties, and other political districts.

10. Having failed to take their heavy liquidation in 1932 and 1933 and to manage successfully "their own affairs," economic and political, the private interests and the state and local political interests, which had once exercised powerful checks on the power and momentum of the Federal Government, lost a large part of their independence; and, as Congress escaped its responsibilities by transferring to the Executive a huge discretionary authority in relation to banking, currency, and spending, centralization proceeded rapidly. In this way the old system of checks and balances, political and economic, was profoundly altered.

11. During this readjustment of financial, credit, currency, banking, and political relationships, organized labor offered no threats to traditional economy or to the efforts made to prevent liquidation, but it did demand, as its price for acquiescence, relief for the unemployed and government support in its effort to force collective bargaining on industry, with a view to securing a larger share of the wealth created under a regime of diminished or fluctuating production, stimulated by government borrowing and spending.

12. In the process of developing its program, in the circumstances described above, the New Deal called into being the elements of a great political "machine," composed of government employees—federal, state, and local (steadily increasing in number), millions of the unemployed dependent on work relief, and state and local officials dependent on grants from the federal Treasury in their efforts to prevent local collapses. Despite federal legislation against political activities on the part of employees and persons sustained by public treasuries, it is a fact that this machine exists and has been used, with a restraint extraordinary in view of the temptations, to keep voters in line behind New Deal policies and to make Senators and Representatives responsive to presidential pressure, particularly when they are up for elections. The phrase "riding into Congress on the President's coat tails" is more than a pleasing euphemism. The establishment of a huge conscript army, with its immense administrative bureaucracy, the rapid expansion of armament industries, and the enactment of new espionage and sedition legislation all conspire to place in Executive hands more power over the life of multitudes. With a political machine, a judicial machine, an industrial machine, and a military machine combined under his control, a President of dictatorial propensities could find ready instruments at hand for extending and entrenching his authority....

BENJAMIN STOLBERG (1891–1951) and WARREN
JAY VINTON (1889–   ) were typical of the
spokesmen of the left who saw in the New Deal a
betrayal of their hopes for fundamental changes in the
structure of American society. Stolberg was a
sociologist, social worker, and labor historian; Vinton
was involved in public housing. Here they spell out
their reasons for judging the New Deal a failure.*

Roosevelt Panaceas

In its attempt to evade the fundamental contradictions of our economy
the New Deal was bound to rely on
panaceas. Its whole program is in essence
nothing but a well-intentioned synthesis
of errors. What it accomplishes in one
direction it undoes in another. It is like
the Russian peasant who cut some cloth
from the front of his pants to patch the
hole in the seat; and then cut from the
leg of his pants to patch the front. After
repeating this operation a dozen times
he wound up, very much like the New
Deal, with his pants all in patches and
the migratory hole still there. (Of course
the Moujik finally got himself a new pair
of pants, but that is another story.)

The Rationalization of Scarcity

The strangest of all the New Deal
illusions is its dream of making Big Ownership accept an economy of abundance.
But, unfortunately for this Utopian vision, capitalism is an economy of measured scarcity. Business is successful to
the extent to which it gauges correctly
that optimum point of profit at which a
maximum price coincides with a maximum demand. And the more nearly it
succeeds in curtailing production at that
point, the better business it is. The vital
concern of Big Industry is to prevent
an abundance of goods from flooding
the market.

---

* From *The Economic Consequences of the New Deal*, copyright, 1935, by Benjamin
Stolberg and Warren Jay Vinton. Reprinted by permission of Harcourt, Brace & World, Inc.

In boom times production is tempted into abundance and scarcity gets out of hand. Capitalist recovery from the ensuing depression lies in the reorganization of scarcity. During the New Era Big Industry blundered into a disastrous abundance. And its potential productivity is now so great that it cannot get out of the depression under its own power. It needed the aid of government to reestablish scarcity and to enforce recovery; and that is exactly what the National Recovery Administration is all about. The codes, avowedly written for the "regulation of competition," are obviously an apparatus for industrial scarcity-mongering.

In order to protect Big Ownership in its scarcity program, the New Deal had to integrate agriculture into the same program. For agriculture during the World War had so increased its production that the collapse of its price structure became a permanent threat to manufacturing prices. And the organization of agricultural scarcity is exactly what the Agricultural Adjustment Administration is all about.

The inner drive of labor, however, is always for greater abundance, for more goods for less money, for shops running at full speed. And so, to integrate labor into this program of anti-social scarcity, the New Deal has been forced, for all its liberal pretensions, to liquidate every expression of labor unrest. And that is exactly why the President insists on a truce between capital and labor, which it is the function of the National Labor Relations Board to achieve.

In short, the first and foremost of the New Deal panaceas, the N.R.A. and the A.A.A., have only served to render more explicit, through an enormous administrative apparatus, what has always been implicit in the nature of Big Ownership. Under capitalism scarcity is the life of trade.

But since it is in the nature of panaceas to mistake their objectives, the New Deal goes right on believing that it is socially planning towards a more abundant life. And to reassure itself it has set up the National Consumers Board, under the chairmanship of the daughter of the Harriman millions, to attempt to undo exactly what the N.R.A. and the A.A.A. were set up to do. The purely academic function of this Board is to organize the notoriously unorganized consumer to brave the massed power of Big Industry in its drive toward scarcity.

Lending for Spending

A vast increase in our internal debt was one of the principal mechanisms through which Big Ownership got us into the depression. And the heroic efforts of millions of debtors to get out of hock on diminished incomes are keeping us there. Yet the New Deal is attempting to get us out of the depression by encouraging further borrowing from Big Ownership on the theory that if only enough people borrow enough money and spend it, business will pick up. (Of course it will—this month—at the expense of next month.)

This attractive theory fits in nicely with the fact that Big Ownership has plenty to lend. Billions are lying idle in the banks. And so in the spring of 1934 the Federal Reserve Board sent out questionnaires to determine how more money might be lent. It received 6,024 replies from banks and Chambers of Commerce. They replied that the smaller manufacturers and business men ought to borrow from the Big Fellows to replenish the capital of which they had been relieved in the depression. They estimated that $662,000,000 could well be used, which would put to work 350,000 people.

With such a host of borrowers in sight it seemed that private banking had been far too cautious in its lending policies. Accordingly the Federal Reserve Banks and the Reconstruction Finance Corporation decided to split up the business between them. Congress authorized the Federal Reserve Banks to make direct loans to industry up to $280,000,000, and it authorized similar loans by the R.F.C. up to $300,000,000. This, said Mr. Eugene Black, then Governor of the Federal Reserve, ought to be "enough for the next year, or the next six months."

It turned out to be far too much. The little fellows refused to bite. Up to the end of October, 1934, they borrowed from the Federal Reserve Banks only $6,226,000 and from the R.F.C. somewhat less than $4,000,000.

In short, industry borrowed less than 2 per cent of the proffered $580,000,000. The little fellows didn't borrow. For one thing, their credit was poor, just as the private bankers had known; and for another they lacked confidence in business revival and rightly feared to get in deeper than they already were. As for big industry, it didn't have to borrow. It has more cash in reserve than it knows what to do with. Those who have the credit have the money, and those who need the money have no credit.

Looking around for another and more likely batch of prospective borrowers the New Deal discovered the American home owners. To be sure, they were already in such a fix that the Home Owners Loan Corporation had had to come to their rescue with $3,000,000,000. They were already in debt up to their necks but not yet in debt up to their ears. A survey was

made to measure this distance, and it was discovered that the home owners needed "repairs and modernization" to the tune of $1,500,000,000. A nation-wide campaign was projected. The New Deal was to do all the propaganda, but the loaning was reserved for the private initiative of the banks. And in order to induce them to loan to such doubtful debtors, the government agreed to insure the banks against loss. It even offered to supply them with funds at 3 per cent, though it allowed them to soak the home owners 9.7 per cent.

But unfortunately, insuring the prospective creditors did not make borrowing any more attractive to the prospective debtors. So far the result of this campaign to increase the business of the banks, to get the construction industry out of its doldrums, and to persuade the American home owner to fix his roof and repair his plumbing has been some $20,000,000 of insured loans.

In short, the lending-for-spending panacea just makes no sense. What the small manufacturers, the little business men, and the home owners really need is to get out debt, not to get deeper into the clutches of Big Ownership. What they need is a redistribution of wealth downwards towards themselves and not further credit from above. They need to get, and not to borrow.

Public Works

The World War was the greatest Public Works project in all history. And when it was over the profits which American Big Ownership had made out of this magnificent project were in part represented by $25,000,000,000 in government bonds which it held as a first lien against the American people. But what most pleased Big Ownership about this wartime project was that the Public Works created by it were immediately shot to hell in defence of its "freedom," and not left over to get funny and compete permanently with private property. The war correlated the destruction of Public Works with their construction.

But a peace-time Public Works project during a capitalist depression is a horse of a very different color. For one thing, such an unreasonably honest administrator as Mr. Ickes sees to it that profits are kept within bounds. Such honesty really amounts to a sabotage of our accustomed modes of doing business. But be that as it may, the real objection on the part of Big Ownership to a peace-time Public Works program—other than the kind which the G.O.P. used to call by the less elegant appellation of the Pork Barrel—is that it must build for permanent use and not for immediate destruction. Such Public Works would become a competitive threat to capital investments.

But the New Deal, with characteristic optimism, slurred over this contradiction in formulating its policy of Public Works. It thought of Public Works primarily as a stimulant to recovery, as a mere "priming of the pump." Naïvely it believed that if it only spent enough, heavy industry would start up again, consumers industries would follow, and business revival would gradually spread. It was Mr. John Maynard Keynes, the well-known English economist, who sold the President this bright idea. He estimated that $300,000,000 a month would turn the trick. But neither he nor anybody else can show just how this will in any way cure our fundamental malady, the maldistribution of wealth and income.

The moment the New Deal started looking for places to spend money it ran headlong into trouble. For one thing,

the field traditionally reserved for government investment—post-offices, bridges, harbors, rivers, roads—had been pretty well exploited by that Great Engineer, Mr. Hoover, in his efforts toward recovery. Nor could the New Deal embark on a program of government-owned means of production, for this field is, of course, the jealously protected preserve of Private Initiative on which no government may poach. Nor could it persuade Big Ownership to borrow from it for expansion, because Big Ownership had already built far more plant and equipment than is workable under our system.

The one great and obvious field in which America has lagged in its physical equipment is housing. The masses of our people need decent, modern, and commodious shelter. And our potential productivity is more than enough to give it to them. During the depression we have wasted through enforced idleness $287,000,000,000 of possible production, far more than enough not only to clean out our slums but to house the American people in the luxury to which their natural resources entitle them. Capitalism has failed to meet this need. It fails to give its workers enough income to pay rent on the present price of modern housing. Nor can it get the cost of modern housing down to present wage levels, for to do so would mean writing down land values, reducing the price of building materials, and giving building labor such steady work that it would be justified in agreeing to a reduction in hourly wage scales.

The New Deal, for all its anxiety to put money into building and construction, has not dared to face these fundamental economic facts. Instead, the New Deal is exerting itself to sustain land values; through the N.R.A. it has been party to a 23 per cent increase in the price of building materials; and, lacking a long-range and extended housing program, it cannot very well ask building labor to reduce its high hourly wage in exchange for a steady annual income. Nor has the New Deal challenged the rate of return on funds invested in housing. It is charging municipalities 4 per cent on the few housing loans it has made, though it has available $1,200,000,-000 of workers' money in its postal savings bank at a cost to itself of only 2 per cent.

The upshot of all the excitement about rehousing the American people has been that the Public Works Administration, out of its $3,700,000,000, has allotted only $146,000,000 for low cost housing. And of this sum only a few millions have actually been spent in eighteen months.

What has happened to the other $3,-554,000,000 which Congress put at Mr. Ickes' disposal?

This amount certainly looks impressive. But an analysis reveals that the New Deal has been using the P.W.A. as a sort of financial clearing house for the routine, though somewhat augmented, work of the various government departments. Every conceivable government agency has been running to Mr. Ickes instead of to Congress for appropriations. The P.W.A. has allotted $277,000,000 to the Navy and $100,000,000 to the Army for strictly military purposes. It has allotted $400,000,000 for traditional federal aid in road building, and $345,-000,000 for the equally traditional federal task of improving rivers and harbors. All told, it has allotted $1,545,000,000 to the regular federal departments for what has been considered routine "public works" ever since the Founding Fathers.

The P.W.A. has also allotted in loans and grants to local governments $789,-000,000 for water works, sewers, street paving, and other traditional local government enterprises. Half the schools in the country are now being built with such P.W.A. funds.

The P.W.A. set aside only $989,000,000 for non-routine federal expenditures. And of this it gave to the late Civil Works Administration $400,000,000 and to the Civilian Conservation Corps $323,-000,000; both of which were essentially make-work projects, and by no stretch of the imagination stimulants to the capital goods industries.

And finally Mr. Ickes also loaned $200,000,000 to the railroads—$54,000,000 more than for housing and called it, in a burst of enthusiasm, Public Works.

Of course a large part of Mr. Ickes' allotments have not yet been spent. And the fact remains that under the New Deal less is being spent on federal and local public works than during the New Era. And as for getting the construction industry out of the depression, it is still dragging along at 30 per cent of normal. Far from "priming the pump" the government has been pouring pail after pail into a well that's gone dry, and then pumping it out again. And if and when it stops pouring in funds, what will happen to the capital goods industries is more than we or the Brain Trust or even Mr. Keynes can tell you.

T.V.A.

The one great war-time Public Works project left over was Muscle Shoals. There it was, enormously visible, in the heart of the Solid South. It was ready to supply a vast region with electricity at low rates and the American farmer with cheap fertilizer. But for fifteen years Big

Ownership fought every attempt to operate Muscle Shoals in competition with itself. And for fifteen years Senator Norris fought to put it to work for the people. Finally in 1933 the New Deal set up the Tennessee Valley Authority to operate Muscle Shoals. But the President went much further.

"It is clear," he said, "that the Muscle Shoals development is but a small part of the potential public usefulness of the entire Tennessee River. Such use, if envisioned in its entirety, transcends mere power development: it enters the wide fields of flood control, soil erosion, afforestation, elimination from agricultural use of marginal lands, and distribution and diversification of industry. *In short, this power development of war days leads logically to national planning for a complete river watershed involving many States and the future lives and welfare of millions. It touches and gives life to all forms of human concerns."* (Italics ours.)

The President's left-wing supporters hailed this promise to correlate social planning with private initiative. And everybody was curious to see how this socialist horse would perform in the capitalist circus.

The experiment started out bravely. Mr. Roosevelt chose three very competent and indubitable progressives to constitute the Authority. And Mr. Ickes blew himself and allotted $50,000,000 to reconstruct the social economy of seven states. Soon the Norris and the Wheeler Dams were under way. Electric distributing lines were brought from public utilities and the supply of electric current was begun. The Authority set up a subsidiary to sell refrigerators and other electric appliances on the installment plan. And it started to build two or three model villages.

But of course Big Ownership could not permit this threat to go unchallenged. The great public utilities retained Newton D. Baker, Wilson's "progressive" Secretary of War, and James M. Beck, former Solicitor-General, to fight the T.V.A. These gentlemen at once came to the unexpected conclusion that the whole experiment was "palpably unconstitutional." And the Southern utilities secured from Federal Judge Grubb in Birmingham a decision which in effect held that the program of the T.V.A. goes far beyond its enabling act; and, moreover, if such a program of social planning had been intended by the act, the act itself would be unconstitutional. In other words, His Honor opined that socialism does not mix with capitalism under the law.

There is no doubt that the T.V.A. means well. Whether it does well is up to the New Deal. If the New Deal steels itself to press for "national planning" in the Tennessee Valley, instead of being content to use the T.V.A. merely as a "yardstick" to measure the just price of a kilowatt hour of electricity, then it can boast that it has offered some challenge to Big Ownership.

We shall see what we shall see. But one thing is certain. The very existence of the T.V.A. is an invaluable lesson to the American people in the possibilities of social control....

The economic consequences of the New Deal have been exactly what might have been foreseen by a competent Brain Trust. Capitalist recovery, on the classic lines of laissez-faire, has not only been impeded but arrested. And its only economic alternative, social planning on socialist lines, has been sedulously avoided.

The New Deal is trying to right the

unbalance of our economic life by strengthening all its contradictions. For Big Ownership it tries to safeguard profits and to keep intact the instruments of its financial domination. For the middle classes it tries to safeguard their small investments, which only serves to reintrench Big Ownership. For labor it tries to raise wages, increase employment, and assure some minimum of economic safety, while at the same time it opposes labor's real interests through its scarcity program. In trying to move in every direction at once the New Deal betrays the fact that it has no policy.

And it has no policy because as a liberal democracy it must ignore the overwhelming fact of our epoch, the irreconcilable conflict between capital and labor. The result is that we are today neither an economy of balanced scarcity, nor an economy of progressive abundance, nor in transit from one to the other. We are today in an economy of stalemate.

During the last year of Mr. Hoover's régime this country was in a state of complete economic disintegration. There was no confidence, there was no hope. Our business structure was collapsing all about us. Finally the banks closed.

When Mr. Roosevelt took office confidence surged back. During its first few months the New Deal staged an inflationary boom. As soon as the bankers returned from their Holiday, Mr. Woodin, then Secretary of the Treasury, sold the public on the idea that the very same credit structure which had collapsed two weeks before had miraculously become sound again. The Administration announced that prices were going to rise, and invited the public to buy while the buying was good. We went off the gold standard, the dollar went down, prices went up, and the public started to buy. Retailers replenished their stocks. Manu-facturers laid in raw materials and began to produce in a hurry before the Blue Eagle could "crack down" on them.

As a result the index of business activity was pumped up in four months from 58 in March, 1933, to 89 in July. There it was punctured abruptly and business activity fell off as rapidly as it had risen. By November it was down to 68. During the first five months of 1934 there was a slow improvement, but by June the increased margins of profits and higher prices of the N.R.A., applied to our anemic purchasing power, began to show their inevitable effects. Business fell off again, and by October, 1934, it was back to 70.

Of course business conditions are somewhat better than they were in the moribund year of 1932. But since June, 1933, there has been no forward progress. Indeed, there has been regression. In October, 1934, which is the last month for which we have available figures, business activity was 2.6 per cent less than a twelvemonth before. Industrial production had declined 6.4 per cent. The steel, lumber, automobile, and textile industries were all less active. Freight car loadings, a sound index of distribution, were 6.1 per cent less. Building construction, measured by value of contracts awarded, was 6.7 per cent lower, despite the heroic efforts of Mr. Ickes to stimulate public works.

When production dropped labor's position naturally worsened. During the same period—from October, 1933, to October, 1934—unemployment increased by 5.4 per cent, while the real weekly wages of industrial workers who still had jobs decreased 2.0 per cent. The number of those on relief increased 33 per cent and the cost of relief almost doubled.

Yet Big Business, with the aid of the N.R.A., has been extracting greatly enlarged profits from our stricken society. Our great industrial corporations increased their profits during the first nine months of 1934 by 76 per cent as against the same period in 1933. According to the *New York Times*, "the chemical companies reported a 45 per cent increase; the mines and metals group, 360 per cent; office equipment, 157 per cent; and tobacco, 166 per cent." And dividends rose 17 per cent in the twelve months ending October, 1934.

When profits rise while wages lag it means but one thing. It means that behind the vivid confusion of the New Deal, the redistribution of the national income is stealthily and fatally progressing *upwards,* and that the power of Big Ownership is steadily enlarging. And unless the goverment succeeds in reversing this disastrous process, Big Ownership is bound to intensify the crisis in the long run.

There is nothing the New Deal has so far done that could not have been done better by an earthquake. A first-rate earthquake, from coast to coast, could have reestablished scarcity much more effectively, and put all the survivors to work for the greater glory of Big Business —with far more speed and far less noise than the New Deal.

ARTHUR M. SCHLESINGER, JR. (1917–   ) is
writing in *The Age of Roosevelt* the major interpretation
of the New Deal as an effort to preserve democracy
from the onslaughts of totalitarianism abroad and an
overpowerful business community at home. Here he
looks at the environment and values that produced the
New Deal. Formerly a professor of history at Harvard,
Schlesinger took a leave of absence to become a
special assistant to President Kennedy.*

Sources of the New Deal

In the background of any historical episode lies all previous history. The strands which a historian may select as vital to an understanding of the particular episode will vary widely according to his interest, his temperament, his faith and his time. Each man must unravel the seamless web in his own way. I do not propose here any definite assessment of the sources of the New Deal. I doubt whether a final assessment is possible. I want rather to call attention to certain possible sources which may not have figured extensively in the conventional accounts, including my own—to the relation of the New Deal to the ebb and flow of American national politics and then

its relation to the international dilemma of free society in this century.

Such relationships are speculative; nonetheless, an attempt to see them may perhaps cast light on some of the less discussed impulses behind the New Deal itself. To begin—and in order to make a sharp issue—let me ask this question: would there have been a New Deal if there had been no depression? Without a depression, would we have had nothing but a placid continuation, so long as prosperity itself continued, of the New Era of the Twenties?

I would answer that there would very likely have been some sort of New Deal in the Thirties even without the Depres-

* Arthur M. Schlesinger, Jr., "Sources of the New Deal; Reflections on the Temper of a Time," *Columbia University Forum*, vol. 2, no. 4 (Fall 1959), pp. 4–12. Reprinted by permission of Columbia University.

sion. I think perhaps our contemporary thinking has come too unreflectively to assume depression as the necessary preliminary for any era of reform. Students of American history know better. The fight against depression was, to be sure, the heart of the New Deal, but it has not been the central issue of traditional American reform: it was not the heart of Jeffersonian democracy nor of Jacksonian democracy nor of the anti-slavery movement nor of the Progressive movement.

What preceded these other epochs of reform was an accumulation of disquietudes and discontents in American society, often non-economic in character, and producing a general susceptibility to appeals for change—this and the existence within society of able men or groups who felt themselves cramped by the status quo and who were capable of exploiting mounting dissatisfaction to advance policies and purposes of their own. This combination of outsiders striving for status and power and a people wearying of the existing leadership and the existing ideals has been the real archetype of American reform.

The official order in the Twenties presented perhaps the nearest we ever came in our history to the identification of the national interest with the interests, values and goals of a specific class—in this case, of course, the American business community. During the generation before Harding, the political leaders who had commanded the loyalties and the energies of the American people—Theodore Roosevelt and Woodrow Wilson—expressed strains in American life distinct from and often opposed to the dominant values of business. They represented a fusion of patrician and intellectual attitudes which saw in public policy

an outlet for creative energy—in Lippmann's phrase, they stood for mastery as against drift. In the service of this conception, they led the people into great national efforts of various sorts, culminating in the convulsive and terrible experience of war. Two decades of this—two decades under the glittering eyes of such leaders as Roosevelt and Wilson, Bryan and La Follette—left the nation in a state of exhaustion.

By 1920 the nation was tired of public crisis. It was tired of discipline and sacrifice. It was tired of abstract and intangible objectives. It could gird itself no longer for heroic moral or intellectual effort. Its instinct for idealism was spent. "It is only once in a generation," Wilson himself had said, "that a people can be lifted above material things. That is why conservative government is in the saddle two-thirds of the time." And the junior official to whom he made this remark, the young Assistant Secretary of the Navy, also noted soon after his unsuccessful try for the Vice-Presidency in 1920, "Every war brings after it a period of materialism and conservatism; people tire quickly of ideals and we are now repeating history." John W. Davis, the Democratic candidate in 1924, said a few years later: "The people usually know what they want at a particular time . . . In 1924 when I was a candidate what they wanted was repose."

A nation fatigued with ideals and longing for repose was ready for "normalcy." As popular attention receded from public policy, as values and aspirations became private again, people stopped caring about politics, which meant that political power inevitably gravitated to society's powerful economic interests—the government of the exhausted nation quite naturally fell to the businessmen.

And for nearly a decade the business government reigned over a prosperous and expanding country.

Yet, for all the material contentment of the Twenties, the decade was also marked by mounting spiritual and psychological discontent. One could detect abundant and multiplying symptoms of what Josiah Royce, after Hegel, used to call a self-estranged social order. The official creed began to encounter growing skepticism, and even opposition and ridicule, in the community at large. Able and ambitious groups, denied what they considered fitting recognition or opportunity, began to turn against the Establishment.

If the economic crash of 1929 astonished the experts, a spiritual crash was diagnosed well in advance. "By 1927," reported Scott Fitzgerald, "a widespread neurosis began to be evident, faintly signalled, like a nervous beating of the feet, by the popularity of crossword puzzles." In the same year Walter Lippmann pointed more soberly to the growing discrepancy between the nominal political issues of the day and the actual emotions of the people. If politics took up these real issues, Lippmann said, it would revolutionize the existing party system. "It is not surprising, then, that our political leaders are greatly occupied in dampening down interest, in obscuring issues, and in attempting to distract attention from the realities of American life."

What was wrong with the New Era was not (as yet) evidence of incompetence or stupidity in public policy. Rather, there was a profound discontent with the monopoly of power and prestige by a single class and the resulting indifference of the national government to deeper tensions. Those excluded from the magic circle suffered boredom, resentment, irritation and eventually indignation over what seemed the intolerable pretensions and irrelevances of their masters. Now it is the gravest error to underrate the power of boredom as a factor in social change. Our political scientists have pointed out convincingly how the human tendency toward inertia sets limits on liberalism; I wish they would spend equal time showing how the human capacity for boredom sets limits on conservatism. The dominant official society —the Establishment—of the Twenties was an exceedingly boring one, neither bright nor witty nor picturesque nor even handsome, and this prodded the human impulse to redress the balance by kicking up heels in back streets.

All this encouraged the defection of specific groups from a social order which ignored their needs and snubbed their ambitions. Within the business community itself there were dissident individuals, especially in the underdeveloped areas of the country, who considered that opportunities for local growth were unduly restrained by Wall Street's control of the money market. The farmers felt themselves shut out from the prevailing prosperity. Elements in the labor movement resented their evident second-class citizenship. Members of foreign nationality groups, especially the newer immigration and its children, chafed under the prevalent assumption that the real America was Anglo-Saxon, Protestant, middle-class and white. In time some of the younger people of the nation began to grow restless before the ideals held out to them; while others, in accepting these ideals, acquired a smug mediocrity which even depressed some of their elders.

Gravest among the symptoms was the

defection of the intellectuals: writers, educators, newspapermen, editors—those who manned the machinery of opinion and who transmitted ideas. The fact of their particular estrangement and discontent guaranteed the articulation, and thus, to a degree, the coordination of the larger unrest. The intellectuals put the ruling class in its place by substituting for its own admiring picture of itself a set of disrespectful images, which an increasing number of people found delightful and persuasive; the insiders, who had before been seen in the reverent terms of Bruce Barton and the *American Magazine,* were now to be seen less reverently through the eyes of H. L. Mencken and Sinclair Lewis. Satire liberated people from the illusion of business infallibility and opened their minds to other visions of American possibility. The next function of the intellectuals was precisely to explore and substantiate those other visions. They did so with zest and ingenuity; and the result was that, beneath the official crust, the Twenties billowed with agitation, criticism and hope. Dewey affirmed man's capability for social invention and management; Beard argued that intelligent national planning was the irresistible next phase in history; Parrington insisted that Jeffersonian idealism had a sound basis in the American past, and indeed expressed a truer Americanism than did materialism. Together the satirists and the prophets drew a new portrait of America—both of the American present and of the American promise—and the increasingly visible discrepancy between what was and what might be in America armed the spreading discontent.

The well of idealism was rising again; energies were being replenished, batteries recharged. Outsiders were pre-paring to hammer on the gates of the citadel. The 1928 election, in which an Irish Catholic challenged Yankee Protestant supremacy, illustrated the gathering revolt against the Establishment. And, though Hoover won the election, Samuel Lubell has pointed out that "Smith split not only the Solid South but the Republican North as well." Smith carried counties which had long been traditionally Republican; he smashed the Republican hold on the cities; he mobilized the new immigrants. In losing, he polled nearly as many votes as Calvin Coolidge had polled in winning four years before. He stood for the vital new tendencies of politics; and it is likely that the prolongation of these tendencies would have assured a national Democratic victory, without a depression, in 1932 or certainly by 1936. And such a Democratic victory would surely have meant the discharge into public life of able and ambitious people denied preference under a business administration —much the same sort of people, indeed, who eventually came to power with the New Deal; and it would have meant new opportunities for groups that had seen the door slammed in their faces in the Twenties—labor, the farmers, the ethnic minorities, the intellectuals.

The suspicion that a political overturn was due even without a depression is fortified, I think, by the calculations of my father in his essay of some years back "The Tides of National Politics." In this essay he proposed that liberal and conservative periods in our national life succeed themselves at intervals of about fifteen or sixteen years; this alternation takes place, he wrote, without any apparent correlation with economic circumstances or, indeed, with anything else, except the ebb and flow of national political psychology. By this argument, a liberal epoch was due in America around 1934 or 1935, depression or no.

In short, the New Deal was, among other things, an expression of what would seem—to use a currently unfashionable concept—an inherent cyclical rhythm in American politics. The Depression did not cause the cycle: what the Depression did was to increase its intensity and deepen its impact by superimposing on the normal cycle the peculiar and unprecedented urgencies arising from economic despair. One might even argue —though I do not think I would—that the Depression coming at another stage in the cycle would not necessarily have produced a New Deal. It is certainly true, as I said, that depressions did not induce epochs of reform in 1873 or in 1893. I think myself, however, that the magnitude of the shock made a political recoil almost certain after 1929. Still, the fact that this recoil took a liberal rather than a reactionary turn may well be due to the accident that the economic shock coincided with a liberal turn in the political cycle.

In any event, the fact remains that the historical New Deal, whether or not something like it might have come along anyway, was after all brought into being by the Depression. It assumed its particular character as it sought to respond to the challenge of economic collapse. And, in confronting this challenge, it was confronting a good deal more than merely an American problem. Mass unemployment touched the very roots of free institutions everywhere. "This problem of unemployment," as Winston Churchill said in England in 1930, "is the most torturing that can be presented to civilized society." The problem was more than torturing; it was something civilized society had to solve if it were to survive. And the issue presented with particular urgency was whether representative democracy could ever deal effectively with it.

Churchill, in the same Romanes lecture at Oxford in 1930, questioned whether it could: democratic governments, he said, drifted along the lines of least resistance, took short views, smoothed their path with platitudes, and paid their way with sops and doles. Parliaments, he suggested, could deal with political problems, but not with economic. "One may even be pardoned," Churchill said, "for doubting whether institutions based on adult suffrage could possibly arrive at the right decisions upon the intricate propositions of modern business and finance." These were delicate problems requiring specialist treatment. "You cannot cure cancer by a majority. What is wanted is a remedy."

The drift of discussion in the United States as well as in Britain in the early Thirties revealed an increasingly dour sense of existing alternatives; on the one hand, it seemed, was parliamentary democracy with economic chaos; on the other, economic authoritarianism with political tyranny. Even more dour was the sense that history had already made the choice—that the democratic impulse was drained of vitality, that liberalism was spent as a means of organizing human action. Consider a selection of statements from American writers at the time, and their mortuary resonance:

The rejection of democracy is nowadays regarded as evidence of superior wisdom. (Ralph Barton Perry)

The moral and intellectual bankruptcy of liberalism in our time needs no demonstration. It is as obvious as rain and as taken for granted. (Nathaniel Peffer)

To attempt a defense of democracy these days is a little like defending paganism in 313 or the divine right of kings in 1793. It is taken for granted that democracy is bad and that it is dying. (George Boas)

'Liberalism is dead.' So many people who seem to agree upon nothing else have agreed to accept these three sweeping words. (Joseph Wood Krutch)

Modern Western civilization is a failure. That theory is now generally accepted. (Louise Maunsell Fields)

Why is it that democracy has fallen so rapidly from the high prestige which it had at the Armistice? . . . Why is it that in America itself—in the very temple and citadel of democracy—self-government has been held up to every ridicule, and many observers count it already dead? (Will Durant)

Only the most venerable among us can remember the creeping fear of a quarter of a century ago that the free system itself had run out of energy, that we had reached, in a phrase Reinhold Niebuhr used as a part of the title of a book in 1934, the "end of an era." What this pessimism implied for the realm of public policy was that democracy had exhausted its intellectual and moral resources, its bag of tricks was played out, and salvation now lay in moving over to a system of total control.

In affirming that there was no alternative between laissez-faire and tyranny, the pessimists were endorsing a passionate conviction held both by the proponents of individualism and the proponents of collectivism. Ogden Mills spoke with precision for American conservatives: "We can have a free country or a socialistic one. We cannot have both. Our economic system cannot be half free and half socialistic. . . . There is no middle ground between governing and being governed, between absolute sovereignty and liberty, between tyranny and free-

dom." Herbert Hoover was equally vehement: "Even partial regimentation cannot be made to work and still maintain live democractic institutions." In such sentiments, Hoover and Mills would have commanded the enthusiastic assent of Stalin and Mussolini. The critical question was whether a middle way was possible—a mixed system which might give the state more power than conservatives would like, enough power, indeed, to assure economic and social security, but still not so much as to create dictatorship. To this question the Hoovers, no less than the Stalins and Mussolinis, had long since returned categorical answers. They all agreed on this, if on nothing else: no.

As I have said, economic planning was not just an American problem. Great Britain, for example, was confronting mass unemployment and economic stagnation; moreover, she had had since 1929 a Labor government. In a sense, it would have been hard to select a better place to test the possibilities of a tranquil advance from laissez-faire capitalism to a managed society. Here was a Labor leadership, sustained by a faith in the "inevitability of gradualness," ruling a nation committed by tradition and instinct to the acceptance of empirical change. How did the British Labor government visualize its problem and opportunity?

The central figures in the Labor government of 1929 were Ramsay MacDonald, now Prime Minister for the second time, and Philip Snowden, his sharp and dominating Chancellor of the Exchequer. Both were classical Socialists who saw in the nationalization of basic industry the answer to all economic riddles. Yet in the existing political situation, with a slim Labor majority, nationalization was out of the question. With socialism excluded, MacDonald and Snowden—indeed, nearly all the Labor party leaders —could see no alternative to all-out socialism but nearly all-out laissez-faire. A capitalist order had to be operated on capitalist principles. The economic policy of the Labor government was thus consecrated as faithfully as that of Herbert Hoover's Republican administration in the United States to the balanced budget and the gold standard—and, far more faithfully than American Republicanism, to free trade.

Socialism across the Channel was hardly more resourceful. As the German Social Democrat Fritz Naphtali put it in 1930, "I don't believe that we can do very much, nor anything very decisive, from the point of view of economic policy, to overcome the crisis until it has run its course." In this spirit of impotence, the democratic Socialists of Europe (until Léon Blum came to power some years later) denied the possibility of a middle way and concluded that, short of full socialization, they had no alternative but to accept the logic of laissez-faire.

The assumption that there were two absolutely distinct economic orders, socialism and capitalism, expressed, of course, an unconscious Platonism—a conviction that the true reality lay in the theoretical essences of which any working economy, with its compromises and confusions, could only be an imperfect copy. If in the realm of essences socialism and capitalism were separate phenomena based on separate principles, then they must be kept rigorously apart on earth. Nor was this use of Platonism—this curious belief that the abstraction was somehow more real than the reality, which Whitehead so well called the "fallacy of misplaced concreteness"—confined to doctrinaire capitalists and doctrinaire social-

ists. The eminent Liberal economist Sir William Beveridge, director of the London School of Economics, braintruster for the Lloyd George welfare reforms before the First World War, spoke for enlightened economic opinion when he identified the "inescapable fatal danger" confronting public policy in the Depression as "the danger of mixing freedom and control. We have to decide either to let production be guided by the free play of prices or to plan it socialistically from beginning to end ... Control and freedom do not mix." Beveridge, encountering Donald Richberg in Washington in the glowing days of 1933, asked a bit patronizingly whether Richberg really believed that there was "a halfway between Wall Street and Moscow." As for Britain, "there is not much that anyone can do now to help us," Beveridge said. "We must plan to avoid another crisis later. We shall not by conscious effort escape this one."

So dogma denied the possibility of a managed capitalism. But could dogma hold out in Britain against the urgencies of depression? Some Englishmen dissented from the either/or philosophy. In the general election of 1929, for example, John Maynard Keynes and Hubert Henderson had provided the Liberal party with the rudiments of an expansionist policy, based on national spending and public works. As unemployment increased in 1930, so too did the pressure for positive government action. That year Sir Oswald Mosley, a member of the Labor government, proposed to a cabinet committee on unemployment an active program of government spending, accompanied by controls over banking, industry and foreign trade. But he could make no impression on the capitalist orthodoxy of the Socialists leaders; Snowden rejected the Mosley memorandum. Another minister suggested leaving the gold standard; Snowden covered him with scorn. To the party conference of 1930, MacDonald said, "I appeal to you to go back to your Socialist faith. Do not mix that up with pettifogging patching, either of a Poor Law kind or Relief Work kind." In other words, socialism meant all or—in this case—nothing!

As economic pressure increased, more and more had to be sacrificed to the balancing of the budget; and the implacable retrenchment meant more governmental economy, reduction in salaries, reduction in normal public works, until, in time, the frenzy for economy threatened the social services and especially the system of unemployment payments on which many British workers relied to keep alive. The summer crisis of 1931, after the failure of *Kreditanstalt*,* weakened the pound; and to Snowden and the Labor government nothing now seemed more essential than staying on the gold standard. To keep Britain on gold required American loans; American loans would not be forthcoming unless satisfactory evidence existed of a determination to balance the budget; and the evidence most likely to satisfy J. P. Morgan and Company, which was arranging the American credit, was a cut in unemployment benefits.

In August 1931, MacDonald and Snowden confronted the cabinet with this dismal logic. Arthur Henderson made it clear that the whole cabinet absolutely accepted Snowden's economic theory: "We ought to do everything in our power to balance the Budget." But MacDonald's proposal for a cut in the dole seemed downright wrong; the Labor government fell. MacDonald soon returned

* Vienna's leading bank, whose failure set off a financial panic in central Europe—Ed.

to office as head of a National government. The new government, slightly more adventurous than its predecessors, took Britain off gold in a few weeks. Sidney Webb, Labor's senior intellectual, provided the Labor government its obituary: "No one ever told *us* we could do that!"

The Labor government having immobilized itself by its intellectual conviction that there was no room for maneuver, no middle way, now succeeded through its collapse in documenting its major premise. Then the experience of 1931 displayed the Right as too hardboiled ever to acquiesce in even the most gradual democratic change. "The attempt to give a social bias to capitalism, while leaving it master of the house," wrote R. H. Tawney, "appears to have failed."

If piecemeal reforms were beyond the power of the Labor government, as they were beyond the desire of a Tory government, then the only hope lay in the rapid achievement of full socialism; the only way socialism could be achieved seemed to be through ruthlessness on the Left as great as that on the Right. Such reasoning was responsible for the lust for catastrophic change that suffused the British Left and infected a part of the American Left in the early Thirties. No one drew more facile and sweeping conclusions than Harold Laski. The fate of the MacDonald government, Laski wrote, was "tantamount to an insistence that if socialists wish to secure a state built upon the principles of their faith, they can only do so by revolutionary means."

From this perspective Laski and those like him quite naturally looked with derision on the advocate of the middle way. In December 1934, for the perhaps somewhat baffled readers of *Redbook* magazine, Laski debated with Maynard Keynes whether America could spend its way to recovery. Public spending, Laski said with horror, would lead to inflation or heavy taxation or waste; it would mean, he solemnly wrote, "an unbalanced budget with the disturbance of confidence (an essential condition of recovery) which this implies": it would bequeath a "bill of staggering dimensions" to future generations. "Government spending as anything more than a temporary and limited expedient," he concluded, "will necessarily do harm in a capitalist society." This was, of course, not only the argument of Ramsay MacDonald but of Herbert Hoover; Laski's novelty was to use it to defend, not a balanced budget and the gold standard, but—socialist revolution.

One way or another, the British Left began to vote against liberal democracy. Sir Oswald Mosley, who had championed the most constructive economic program considered within the MacDonald government, indicated the new direction when, with John Strachey and others, he founded the authoritarian-minded New Party in 1931. Mosley's excesses soon led him toward fascism and discredit; but plenty of others were reaching similar conclusions about the impossibility of reform under capitalism. Sidney and Beatrice Webb abandoned Fabianism for the mirage of a new civilization in the Soviet Union. All peaceful roads to progress seemed blocked. After a visit with Roosevelt in Washington, Cripps wrote, "My whole impression is of an honest anxious man faced by an impossible task—humanizing capitalism and making it work." The one thing that is not inevitable now," said Cripps, "is gradualness."

Both Right and Left—Hoover and Stalin, John W. Davis and Mussolini,

Ogden Mills and Stafford Cripps—thus rejected the notion of a socially directed and managed capitalism, of a mixed economy, of something in between classical free enterprise and classical socialism. And the either/or demonstration commanded considerable respect in the United States—self-evidently on the American Right; and to some degree on the American Left. So Laski had made clear in *Democracy in Crisis* that the American ruling class would be as tough and hopeless as any other:

> What evidence is there, among the class which controls the destiny of America, of a will to make the necessary concessions? Is not the execution of Sacco and Vanzetti, the long indefensible imprisonment of Mooney, the grim history of American strikes, the root of the answer to that question?

In 1932 both Right and Left thus stood with fierce intransigence on the solid ground of dogma. In so doing, they were challenging an essential part of the American liberal tradition. When Professor Rexford G. Tugwell of the Columbia University economics department, on leave in Washington, revisited his campus in 1933, he rashly bragged of the New Deal's freedom from "blind doctrine," and the *Columbia Spectator,* then edited by a brilliant young undergraduate named James Wechsler, seized on this boast as the fatal weakness of Tugwell's argument and of the whole New Deal. "This is the crux of the problem," the *Spectator* said; "the blind stumbling in the most chaotic fashion—experimenting from day to day—without any anchor except a few idealistic phrases—is worthless. It is merely political pragmatism."

Merely political pragmatism—to ideologists, whether of Right or of Left, this seemed conclusive evidence of intellectual bankruptcy. As the conservatives had said that any attempt to modify the capitalist system must mean socialism, so the radicals now said that any attempt to maintain the capitalist system must mean fascism. "Roosevelt's policies can be welded into a consistent whole," wrote I. F. Stone, "only on the basis of one hypothesis . . . that Mr. Roosevelt intends to move toward fascism." "The essential logic of the New Deal," wrote Max Lerner, "is increasingly the naked fist of the capitalist state."

Convinced of the fragility of the system, the radicals saw themselves as the forerunners of apocalypse. "American commercial agriculture is doomed," wrote Louis Hacker; capitalism was doomed, too, and the party system, and the traditional American way of life. In 1934 Sidney Hook, James Burnham, Louis Budenz, V. F. Calverton, James Rorty and others addressed "An Open Letter to American Intellectuals." "We cannot by some clever Rooseveltian trick," the letter warned,

evade the unfolding of basic economic and political developments under capitalism . . . Let us not deceive ourselves that we shall not have to face here also the choice between reaction, on the one hand, and a truly scientific economy under a genuine workers' democracy on the other.

In 1935 *The New Republic* stated with magisterial simplicity the argument of the radicals against the New Dealers, of New York against Washington, of the Marxists against the pragmatists.

Either the nation must put up with the confusions and miseries of an essentially unregulated capitalism, or it must prepare to supersede capitalism with socialism. *There is no longer a feasible middle course.*

Both radicalism and conservatism thus ended in the domain of either/or. The contradictions of actuality, which so stimulated the pragmatists of Washington, only violated the proprieties and offended the illusions of the ideologists. While they all saw themselves as hardheaded realists, in fact they were Platonists, preferring essence to existence and considering abstractions the only reality.

The great central source of the New Deal, in my judgment, lay precisely in the instinctive response of practical, energetic, and compassionate people to those dogmatic absolutes. This passion to sacrifice reality to doctrine presented a profound challenge to the pragmatic nerve. Many Americans, refusing to be intimidated by abstractions or to be overawed by ideology, responded by doing things. The whole point of the New Deal lay in its belief in activism, its faith in gradualness, its rejection of catastrophism, its indifference to ideology, its conviction that a managed and modified capitalist order achieved by piecemeal experiment could combine personal freedom and economic growth. "In a world in which revolutions just now are coming easily," said Adolf Berle, "the New Deal chose the more difficult course of moderation and rebuilding." "The course that the new Administration did take," said Harold Ickes, "was the hardest course. It conformed to no theory, but it did fit into the American system—a system of taking action step by step, a system of regulation only to meet concrete needs, a system of courageous recognition of change." Tugwell, rejecting laissez-faire and communism, spoke of the "third course."

Roosevelt himself, of course, was the liberal pragmatist *par excellence*. His aim was to steer between the extremes of chaos and tyranny by moving always, in his phrase, "slightly to the left of center." "Unrestrained individualism" he wrote, had proved a failure; yet "any paternalistic system which tries to provide for security for everyone from above only calls for an impossible task and a regimentation utterly uncongenial to the spirit of our people." He constantly repeated Macaulay's injunction to reform if you wished to preserve.

Roosevelt had no illusions about revolution. Mussolini and Stalin seemed to him, in his phrase, "not mere distant relatives" but "blood brothers." When Emil Ludwig asked him his "political motive," he replied, "My desire is to obviate revolution . . . I work in a contrary sense to Rome and Moscow." He said during the 1932 campaign:

Say that civilization is a tree which, as it grows, continually produces rot and dead wood. The radical says: 'Cut it down.' The conservative says: 'Don't touch it.' The liberal compromises: 'Let's prune, so that we lose neither the old trunk nor the new branches.' This campaign is waged to teach the country to march upon its appointed course, the way of change, in an orderly march, avoiding alike the revolution of radicalism and the revolution of conservatism.

I think it would be a mistake to underestimate the extent to which this pragmatic attitude was itself a major source of New Deal vitality. The exaltation of the middle way seems banal and obvious enough today. Yet the tyranny of dogma was such in the early years of the Great Depression that infatuation with ideology blocked and smothered the instinctive efforts of free men to work their own salvation. In a world intoxicated with abstractions, Roosevelt and the New Dealers stood almost alone in a stubborn faith in rational experiment, in trial and error. No one understood this more keenly than the great English critic of absolutes; Keynes, in an open letter to Roosevelt at the end of 1933, stated the hopes generated by the New Deal with precision and eloquence. "You have made yourself," Keynes told Roosevelt,

the trustee for those in every country who seek to mend the evils of our condition by reasoned experiment within the framework of the existing social system. If you fail, rational choice will be gravely prejudiced throughout the world, leaving orthodoxy and revolution to fight it out. But, if you succeed, new and bolder methods will be tried everywhere, and we may date the first chapter of a new economic era from your accession to office.

The question remains: why did the New Deal itself have the pragmatic commitment? Why, under the impact of depression, was it not overborne by dogma as were most other governments and leaders in the world? The answer to this lies, I suspect, in the point I proposed earlier—in the suggestion that the New Deal represented, not just a response to depression, but also a response to pent-up frustration and needs in American society—frustrations and needs which would have operated had there been no depression at all. The periodic demand for forward motion in American politics, the periodic breakthrough of new leadership—these were already in the works before the Depression. Depression, therefore, instead of catching a nation wholly unprepared, merely accelerated tendencies toward change already visible in the national community. The response to depression, in short, was controlled and tempered by the values of traditional American experimentalism, rather than those of rigid ideology. The New Deal was thus able to approach the agony of mass unemployment and depression in the pragmatic spirit, in the spirit which guaranteed the survival rather than the extinction of freedom, in the spirit which in time rekindled hope across the world that free men could manage their own economic destiny.

If Europeans like Isaiah Berlin saw Roosevelt's
New Deal as a massive effort to preserve democracy,
others saw it in a darker perspective. The French
journalist AMAURY DE RIENCOURT (1918–)
argues that the modern world, like ancient Rome, has
drifted into a Caesarian totalitarianism and that the
New Deal was the American version of this general
phenomenon.*

Caesarism Comes to America

... The election of Franklin Roosevelt in 1932 was a major turning point in the history of America, and indirectly of the world. America elected a new tribune of the people, a tribune who was no longer the captive of business and vested interests but one who felt responsible to the entire nation. He was a Democrat but also the champion of a revolt that had started forty years before under the Populists' leadership and had often cut across party lines. Conscious of this national rather than merely partisan backing, Franklin Roosevelt was determined to establish a semidictatorial rule, a personal rule such as none of his strong predecessors would have dared contemplate in their wildest dreams. He had no wish to carry out a revolution and explained quite clearly that no such revolution was necessary: "Our Constitution is so simple and practical that it is possible always to meet extraordinary needs by changes in emphasis and arrangement without loss of essential form. . . ."

... Victorious democrats often seem to find their greatest leaders among the remnants of former aristocracies in whom lurks the intense if unconscious dislike for money-making and sheer plutocracy. This pattern was quite in evidence in Rome among the intensely aristocratic leaders of Roman democracy: the Gracchi, Drusus, and Caesar. It was just as

* Reprinted by permission of Coward-McCann, Inc., from *The Coming Caesars* by Amaury de Riencourt. Copyright © 1957 by Amaury de Riencourt.

evident in the selection of Franklin Delano Roosevelt. It is these aristocratic leaders who, having been raised in an atmosphere of social privilege, apart from the people, can be moved by popular misfortune because they are not part of it but look at it from the outside. Belonging to a respectable squirearchy settled along the Hudson River, possessing wealth that made it easy for him to despise something he had never lacked, Franklin Roosevelt could let his generous impulses guide him uncritically He despised money because he did not understand it. Although this attitude gave him the immense appeal of a true tribune, it colored his economic views with a dangerous amateurishness. Under his leadership, the New Deal was to engineer a great social revolution but would not solve the basic problem of a depression which threatened to become chronic. World War II finally put an end to it by mobilizing all the immense resources of a nation that seemed to have too much for full use in peacetime. . . .

Throughout the first year of his rule, Roosevelt concentrated an increasing amount of power in his hands, overriding the reluctance of a disgruntled Congress. Administrative agencies assumed a degree of power and independence that left the legislative branch with very little influence on the dizzy course of events. Final decisions rested with a President who handled his huge power with increasing assurance as time went on. Roosevelt was not carrying out a constitutional revolution, as his enemies asserted, but was merely leading America back to the one and only path along which her history had been proceeding: the path toward growing executive power. It was not a fresh start but the fulfillment of a profound trend whose origin lay deep in the past. All those

who deplored the trend, who lamented the waning of the former "rugged individualism," were belated romanticists who refused to move with the times. The spirit of the Roman *panem et circenses* was slowly pervading the atmosphere, without destroying the willingness to work but weakening the former self-reliance of pioneering days. The mainstay of American freedom—freedom *from* authority—began to give way now that a large majority of the people were willing to barter freedom for security.

The psychological change was profound and it made the emergence of an all-powerful, paternalistic state inevitable. It was not this Welfare State that weakened the individual's self-reliance, as its critics contend. The Welfare State merely sanctioned what had become a fact, a psychological change of profound scope, to which it adapted new social and economic institutions. The emergence of the Welfare State as a controlling apparatus, operating both on a gigantic scale and in a minutely differentiated field, was as much a result as a contributing cause of the gradual decline in the average individual's self-reliance and initiative. Individual man was increasingly trapped in the complex network of a colossal machinery of which he saw and understood only a very small part. This psychological evolution indicated a change of historical phase in the individual's outlook, from the dynamic to the static. Dwarfed by the size and complexity of modern society, he became willing to surrender a large part of his stimulating but dangerous freedom for the sake of economic security. It was all in the cards that Franklin Roosevelt did not make but which he dealt with consummate skill. His leadership was not collective but intensely personal. He consulted many men but always made his own decisions alone. Nothing could have been further removed from a parliamentary type of government. The New Deal "brain trusts" were unique in their conception, a typical American creation attempting to mechanize and mass-produce ideas by pooling human minds. But they had nothing in common with parliamentary debates. They operated like general staffs under military discipline. Only the Commander in Chief was entitled to make decisions and he did not have to give any explanations. He was like another typical American creation, the master-mind sports coach who bosses his team, devises its tactics and strategy, switches players and substitutes at will. However, endowed with true political genius like all Caesarian figures, Roosevelt always knew how to give to the American people the feeling that his power and his decisions were theirs.

Much has been and will be written about Franklin Roosevelt's exceedingly complex character, his courage and yet his evasiveness, his idealism and his acute realism. Mommsen's succinct summing up of Julius Caesar's character—"the most supple master of intrigue"—is perhaps the most fitting description of Roosevelt. What Roosevelt had to a supreme degree was a charismatic charm that poured out naturally, the irresistible charm of a born leader of men. As soon as he was in office he communicated with the American people through his "fireside chats," a remarkable exercise in mass hypnotism. The fact that he came, in time, to have the major part of the press against him did not make a dent in his popular appeal. A new, device, the radio, had prevailed over the older printed word; and when his magnetic voice purred its way into the ears of millions of his compatriots, he managed to cast an unbreakable spell on America.

Logical argumentation could no longer prevail, as it had in the days of the Founding Fathers. Political speeches had already long ago become what rhetoric and diatribe had become in the Classical world when they displaced eloquence: they were used for effect, not for content. They conjured emotions but did not appeal to the intellect; and at this game, Franklin Roosevelt was unrivaled.

The greatest reward of this projection of one man's warm personality on the national consciousness was a remarkable recrudescence of confidence which economic circumstances did not really warrant—and many political opponents were quick to point out the numerous flaws in the Administration's policy. But against Roosevelt's personality, conservatives were as powerless as radical demagogues like Huey Long. The Caesarian flavor of this highly personal rule was partly masked from his contemporaries by the easygoing familiarity of the man. As a New Dealer remarked: "The New Deal is a laughing revolution. It is purging our institutions in the fires of mockery, and it is led by a group of men who possess two supreme qualifications for the task: common sense and a sense of humor." Certainly this leadership was closer to that of popular pre-Caesarian Rome than it was to the Wagnerian tyranny of Germany's Nazism with its terrifying *Götterdämmerung* atmosphere. But its humane humorous aspect was only a mask, a psychological compensation for the almost absolute power behind it. It was not issued of a brutal revolution as was the fashion in the unstable worlds of the Hellenes and the Europeans; it was the actualization of an old trend and those who lived through it and trembled for the safety of their republican institutions could always attempt to comfort themselves by pointing out its familiar, even traditional features. But the lengthening shadow of growing Caesarism was unmistakably there.

Another source of Roosevelt's power was in his knowledge of how to handle the political world, Congress especially. He was a consummate politician whose leadership within his party could no longer be challenged, who used patronage with considerable effectiveness. Skill in handling Congress and full use of his veto power gave him, in fact, almost unlimited influence on lawmaking, thanks to the fact that he always had the initiative. It was all strictly constitutional and yet the separation of powers so fondly cherished by the Founding Fathers was no more than a ghost by then.

The New Deal implied simultaneous relief and recovery, and then profound reform of the economic and social structure. The speed with which the new Administration went to work on relief reduced Congress to the position of a rubber-stamping body. Individual Senators could hurl the epithet "dictator" at the President but the country at large trusted its tribune and repeatedly voted him back in office. Time and again, Congress was asked to vote huge sums of money without being given even a minimum of information as to how and by what organization the spending was to be carried out. Roosevelt's control over the fast-expanding network of agencies and committees was masterful and often left his closest advisers as much in the dark as regards his grand strategy as the Congressmen themselves.

Sixty different agencies were involved in relief undertakings and only the President knew all the twists, detours, and corners of his administrative labyrinth. The best example of his shrewd handling of men was his creation of two opposed and yet complementary agencies with confusing initials: Hopkins' W.P.A. and Ickes' P.W.A.—always quarreling, yet always forced into close collaboration by the White House's imperious arbitration.

Washington gradually became the seat of the world's greatest business enterprise: the Administration of the United States. A strange new world came into being, dwarfing and shattering the prestige of the old business world of bankers and industrial magnates. It was a world of pure politics and bureaucracy emancipated from business control, a world in which men competed for power and prestige, not for financial profits, a world of mandarins and brain-trust intellectuals. For the first time in the history of the United States, the despised intellectual reached a position of substantial power and even respectability. The American intellectual, the psychological "freedman" of the modern world, began his real emancipation under Franklin Roosevelt as Rome's equally despised intellectual freedmen (mostly of Greek extraction) reached power when Julius Caesar established his permanent bureaucracy after the downfall of Roman Big Business.

All this bewildered the former rulers of the country whose only world outlook was financial profit, who looked down upon politics as the handmaid of private business, and who bitterly resented their new master. And from the opposite direction left-wing radicals struck out at Roosevelt for not doing away with capitalism altogether. But he stood his ground, acting as a surgeon, not as an executioner.

Congress had been more or less disposed of, but across Roosevelt's path stood an old-fashioned, defiant judiciary that carried over into the new age the old limited views, the lack of comprehension that had made it for so long an unthinking ally of Big Business. A strong President always ends by clashing with the Supreme Court, but Roosevelt's clash was momentous. In 1935 the Supreme Court found that the National Industrial Recovery Act was unconstitutional because it granted too many legislative powers to the President; other acts were soon invalidated by the same judicial procedure. Emboldened by his tremendous success at the polls in 1936, Roosevelt overreached himself with his Supreme Court "packing" scheme—Congress refused to sanction it. But the Justices had been impressed by the demonstration of electoral will as well as alarmed by this undisguised threat to their autonomy. The Court virtually capitulated and approved the National Industrial Recovery Act—and with this the executive branch moved boldly into the legislative arena and carved out for itself an absolute predominance over the "fourth branch" that was coming into being: the autonomous agencies and commissions such as the Tennessee Valley Authority in which executive, legislative, and judiciary powers were inextricably intertwined. Henceforth the political parties were no longer the sole connective tissue joining together the separate powers of government. A new autonomous bureaucracy under executive control towered over them.

Like all the great reformers in Rome, Franklin Roosevelt had incurred at first the almost unanimous hostility of lawyers and jurists, always the first to react to arbitrary modes of procedure; and if he could always overpower Congress, he had to tread gingerly when it came to dealing with the conservative-minded judi-

cial element. But he finally reached his goal by dint of skill and patience. He was eventually able, because of vacancies, to appoint seven out of nine members of the Supreme Court and reshape it decisively. The legal profession finally made its peace with the New Deal and provided many of its administrative brains, emphasizing the pragmatic nature of the great experiment with its reliance on American "legal realism," case law rather than logical legal philosophy, applied law rather than theoretical....

The New Deal was in line with American tradition. It was essentially concrete-minded and pragmatic. It concentrated on practical issues, not on theoretical formulations; but although it alleviated the worst features of the Great Depression, it proved unable to cure the more fundamental national ills. Roosevelt's violent campaign speeches in 1936 frightened and antagonized the business community needlessly, and made a lasting reconciliation with the business managers impossible.

... The rise of democratic political power in Rome took place, as it did in America, through the big political machines. The corrupt rule of ring-and-bossdom in an elective democracy is almost inevitable. Franklin Roosevelt's strength lay in his shrewd manipulation of the big city Democratic machines, not in the national Democratic party as such. National parties, agglomerations of discordant local interests without specific doctrine and philosophy, were and are increasingly dominated by the "indispensable man." Vitality resides in the local organizations, not in their federal structure. Roosevelt could fight relentlessly against Huey Long's machine in Louisiana and James Curley's machine in Massachusetts. But he could only do so successfully by depending on a majority of the other machines. His alliance with Edward Flynn, boss of the Bronx, was comparable to Caesar's reliance on Clodius' machine against Milo's "Tammany Hall." Clodius' machine was primarily a vote-buying organization that distributed free wheat to its clientele, standing on a platform advocating the emancipation of slaves and freedom for Roman labor to organize itself.

But centralization is greater in America than it was in Rome, in a sense at least. Political power is more concentrated in the one elected tribune instead of being parceled out among many officials af equal rank as was the case in Rome. So it was that Roosevelt was able to dominate most local machines by making the W.P.A. itself into a gigantic, nation-wide supermachine with extensive political ramifications. The vote-buying that characterizes local machines was applied on a federal scale and paid rich dividends to the Roosevelt Administration. From now on, this federal dwarfing of such petty machines as Tammany Hall became a prime factor in American politics. A great deal of the political credit still granted to local organizations depends on their ability to obtain funds from the federal treasury rather than on their own local resources. . . .

Under Franklin Roosevelt's New Deal, America took a decisive step toward Caesarism. The remarkable feature of this subtle evolution was that it could take place constitutionally, without any illegal move, simply by stretching the extremely pliable fabric of America's political institutions. Romans had a far greater distrust of concentrated power than the Americans and they had so fragmented political authority that any

man who aspired to full executive power had to hold, simultaneously and unconstitutionally, the official positions of Consul, Proconsul, Tribune, Quaestor, Censor, and Pontifex Maximus—never forgetting that each one of those offices, save the last, was split between several incumbents. In America, the existence of the Presidency makes the transition far easier and wholly constitutional. Where constitutional obstacles appear insurmountable—the hostility of the Supreme Court, mostly—intimidation can usually be just as effective if it is backed by public opinion. Roosevelt was quick to point this out when he insisted in the autumn of 1937 that the Supreme Court had been "forced" into line after his threatening message in February of the same year.

It is essential to keep in mind that all this is the result of profound historical trends, not of any one man's dictatorial ambitions. Circumstances, not conscious desires, create Caesarism. In the case of America, it is clear that psychological reasons favor this historical evolution. Americans are hero worshipers to a far greater extent than any European people. Concrete-minded and repelled by the abstract, they always tend to personalize issues, and in every walk of life they look up to the "boss." They are led by insensible degrees to foster a Caesarism that historical evolution favors anyway. A friend of Roosevelt's could write with great perception: "For one who knows the President it is impossible to believe that he is aiming at a future dictatorship; but it is also impossible not to recognize the packing of the Supreme Court as exactly what a dictator would adopt as his first step. The President may not know where he is going, but he is on his way.". . .

SAMUEL LUBELL (1911–   ) is one of a breed of new social analysts who rely heavily on research devices such as systematic public opinion polling. A newspaperman and columnist, Lubell in *The Future of American Politics* (1951) and *Revolt of the Moderates* (1956) has offered a fresh and imaginative interpretation of the nature of modern American politics. He finds that changes in the ethnic makeup, urban-rural distribution, and socio-economic aspirations of the American people have been the determinants of political patterns.*

Revolt of the City

A Little Matter of Birth Rates

[T]he growing up of [the] children of the 13,000,000 immigrants who poured into the country between 1900 and 1914 was bound to exert a leveling pull on American society. As it was, the depression—striking when most of them had barely entered the adult world—sharpened all their memories of childhood handicaps. When Roosevelt first took office, no segment of the population was more ready for "a new deal" than the submerged, inarticulate urban masses. They became the chief carriers of the Roosevelt Revolution.

The really revolutionary surge behind the New Deal lay in this coupling of the depression with the rise of a new generation, which had been malnourished on the congestion of our cities and the abuses of industrialism. Roosevelt did not start this revolt of the city. What he did do was to awaken the climbing urban masses to a consciousness of the power in their numbers. He extended to them the warming hand of recognition, through patronage and protective legislation. In the New Deal he supplied the leveling philosophy required by their sheer numbers and by the hungers stimulated by advertising. In turn, the big-city masses furnished the votes which reelected Roosevelt again and again—and, in the process, ended the traditional Republican majority in this country....

* From pp. 28–57, *The Future of American Politics* by Samuel Lubell. Copyright 1951, 1952 by Samuel Lubell. Reprinted by permission Harper & Row, Publishers.

There were two population currents which cleared the way for the New Deal:

Between 1910 and 1930 for the first time a majority of the American people came to live in cities. The second population shift might be described as the triumph of the birth rates of the poor and underprivileged over those of the rich and well born. . . .

Nor was it the birth rates of the immigrants alone which were threatening the Republican majority. The other prolific baby patches were in the farming areas, particularly in the Appalachian hills and in the South. When World War One shut off the flow of European immigrants, it was into these areas of high human fertility and low living standards that industry sent its recruiting agents searching for cheap labor. Whites and Negroes were sucked north into the cities, especially after 1920 when immigration was curtailed sharply.

Between 1920 and 1930 more than 6,-500,000 persons were drawn off the farms and hills; 4,500,000 came into New York, Chicago, Detroit and Los Angeles alone. They hit the cities at roughly the same time that the children of the immigrants were growing up and bestirring themselves. The human potential for a revolutionary political change had thus been brought together in our larger cities when the economic skies caved in.

Through the entire Roosevelt era the Republicans labored on the wrong side of the birth rate. Nor was there anything they could do about it, since the birth rates frustrating them were those of 1910 to 1920. During the last years of Republican victory, from 1920 through 1928, roughly 17,000,000 potential new voters passed the age of twenty-one. From 1936 through 1944, the number ran over 21,-000,000, most of them coming from poorer, Democratically inclined families.

Whatever inroads into Roosevelt's popularity the Republicans made was offset largely by these new voters. In 1936, for example, nearly 6,000,000 more ballots were cast than in 1932. While the Republicans gained just under 1,000,000, Roosevelt's vote swelled by almost 5,000,000. . . .

Never having known anything but city life, this new generation was bound to develop a different attitude toward the role of government from that of Americans born on farms or in small towns. To Herbert Hoover the phrase "rugged individualism" evoked nostalgic memories of a rural self-sufficiency in which a thrifty, toiling farmer had to look to the marketplace for only the last fifth of his needs. The Iowa homestead on which Hoover grew up produced all of its own vegetables, its own soap, its own bread. Fuel was cut and hauled from the woods ten miles away, where one could also gather walnuts free. "Sweetness" was obtained from sorghums. Every fall the cellar was filled with jars and barrels which, as Hoover observes in his memoirs, "was social security in itself."

To men and women who regulated their labors by the sun and rain, there was recognizable logic in talking of natural economic laws—although even among farmers the murmur for government intervention grew louder, as their operations became more commercialized and less self-sufficient.

In the city, though, the issue has always been man against man. What bowed the backs of the factory worker prematurely was not hardships inflicted by Mother Nature but by human nature. He was completely dependent on a money wage. Without a job, there were no vegetables for his family, no bread, no rent, no fuel, no soap, no "sweetness." Crop failures, plagues of grasshoppers or searing drought could be put down as acts of God. Getting fired or having one's wages cut were only too plainly acts of the Boss.

A philosophy that called for "leaving things alone" to work themselves out seemed either unreal or hypocritical in the cities, where nearly every condition of living groaned for reform. The wage earner had to look to the government to make sure that the milk bought for his baby was not watered or tubercular; he had to look to government to regulate the construction of tenements so all sunlight was not blocked out. If only God could make a tree, only the government could make a park.

Neither the Republicans nor the New Dealers seem to have appreciated how sharp a wrench from the continuity of the past was involved in the rise of this big-city generation. G.O.P. leaders persisted in regarding Roosevelt's popularity as a form of hero worship, abetted by the radio. Only Roosevelt's personal magnetism and political skill were holding together the varied Democratic elements, reasoned the Republicans. With "that voice" quieted, the coalition would fall apart. The nation would then return to safe and sane Republicanism. What this reasoning overlooked was that the Roosevelt generation had no tradition of Republicanism to go back to. For them the weight of tradition was such that if they were undecided about rival Presidential candidates, they instinctively would give the Democrats preference.

The basic weakness of the Republican party stems from this fact, that it remains rooted in an earlier historical era in which it was dominant. The resilient Democratic strength springs from being so alive—clumsily perhaps, but definitely alive—to the problems with which the newer generation has grown up.

Between the Republican and Democratic appeals, as we shall see, the issue is less one of conservatism versus liberalism than one of timeliness.

The Forgotten Warrior

At the height of Roosevelt's popularity, Republicans used to lament over the youthfulness of so many of the nation's voters. Since they had come of age since 1928, the complaint ran, the only Presidents they knew were Roosevelt and Hoover, who was hopelessly linked with the depression. Still, it would be a mistake to regard the Roosevelt coalition as strictly a product of the depression.

The startling fact—generally overlooked—is that through the booming twenties Republican pluralities in the large industrial centers were dropping steadily. Even when the stock market tickers were clicking most gratifyingly the forces of urban revolt were gathering momentum.

Consider the waning Republican strength revealed in the table below which totals the vote in our twelve largest cities (New York, Chicago, Philadelphia, Pittsburgh, Detroit, Cleveland, Baltimore, St. Louis, Boston, Milwaukee, San Francisco and Los Angeles). In 1920 the Republicans had 1,638,000 more votes than the Democrats in these twelve cities. This net Republican plurality dropped in 1924 and was turned into a Democratic plurality by 1928.

Year	Net Party Plurality	
1920	1,638,000	Republican
1924	1,252,000	Republican
1928	38,000	Democratic
1932	1,910,000	Democratic
1936	3,608,000	Democratic
1940	2,210,000	Democratic
1944	2,296,000	Democratic
1948	1,443,000	Democratic

Two things stand out from those figures. First, it was not the depression which made Roosevelt the champion of the urban masses but what he did after he came to the Presidency. Between 1932 and 1936 the Democratic plurality in these cities leaped 80 per cent, the biggest change in any single election. Second, the Republican hold on the cities was broken not by Roosevelt but by Alfred E. Smith. Before the Roosevelt Revolution there was an Al Smith Revolution. . . .

So overwhelming was Roosevelt's 1936 victory, that its political decisiveness is often overlooked. With only Maine and Vermont remaining Republican, Roosevelt's re-election seemed primarily a vote of gratitude for lifting the country out of a desperate economic crisis. Certainly many people favored him for that reason. But 1936 was also the year of realignment in which the Democrats became the nation's normal majority party. The traditional dominance which the Republicans had enjoyed since the Civil War was washed away and a new era in American politics began.

The depression vote of 1932 still mirrored the orbit of conflict of the old Republican order. The G.O.P. cleavage had been mainly a struggle between the "progressives" of the Midwest and Far West against the industrial East. Roosevelt's first campaign was directed primarily toward splitting off this "progressive" vote. His best showing came in the Western and Mountain states. All six states he lost—Pennsylvania, Delaware, Connecticut, Vermont, New Hampshire and Maine—were in the East.

The shift in the basis of Roosevelt's appeal "from acreage to population," to use Raymond Moley's phrase, occurred in 1935. Moley credits the change to Huey Long's "Share Our Wealth" agitation and to Roosevelt's ire over the Supreme Court's declaring the N.R.A. un-

constitutional. To steal Long's thunder, Roosevelt proposed a "soak the rich" tax bill, which, Moley feels, marked the beginning of the conservative-liberal split inside the Democratic party. Whatever the exact turning point, 1935 saw more social legislation enacted than in any other year in the nation's history—the "wealth tax," the Wagner Labor Relations Act, the Social Security Law, the creation of WPA, the Public Utilities Holding law, the start of the Rural Electrification Administration.

Not only in Washington but throughout the country 1935 was the year of decision. To go back to the old order or to move forward to something different? That was the question posed for decision in 1935, in countless different ways, in every phase of life.

In the early New Deal days how things were done had been less important than getting the stalled economy going again. By 1935 recovery had progressed to the point where there no longer was any question that the country would be saved. The new issue was: Would the "good old days" of unchallenged business dominance be restored? Or was America to be reshaped?

The more articulate business groups had one answer . . . they were ready to resume their annual Chamber of Commerce dinners as if there never had been a depression. But the same processes of recovery which restored the courage of businessmen also enabled the leaders of organized labor to recover their nerve. Early in 1933 John L. Lewis, Phil Murray and Tom Kennedy lamented to Roosevelt that the United Mine Workers had barely enough members to pay the union's expenses. "Go home and have a good night's sleep," Roosevelt consoled them. "If I don't do anything else in my administration I am going to give the miners an opportunity to organize in the United Mine Workers of America."

Taking Roosevelt at his word, Lewis nearly emptied the UMW treasury to hire organizers, sending them out to tell the miners, "The President wants you to join a union." By 1934 Lewis could stand before the A. F. of L. convention and boast that the UMW was again a fighting force of 400,000 miners. By 1935 he was ready to demand that the A. F. of L. embrace the principle of industrial unionism or let a new labor movement organize the mass production industries.

The hard right to the jaw which Lewis swung at Bill Hutcheson in Atlantic City that October was symbolic of the fact that at least one group of labor leaders were determined not to go back to the old order.

When the first sit-down strike broke in November 1935, it came—significantly—not among workers of immigrant origin, but among the rubber workers of Akron. That city had drawn so many hillbillies from near-by states that it was often jokingly called "the capital of West Virginia." Before taking their place in the picket line, some rubber workers knelt in prayer. After the last "Amen," they picked up their baseball bats and lead pipes and moved into formation around the factories.

This fervor for unions which swept the native American workers—some observers likened it to a religious revival—was of crucial political importance. Al Smith, as we have seen, stirred a new sense of political consciousness among workers of immigrant and Catholic origin. But the native workers off the farms and hills had always held suspiciously aloof from those of immigrant stock.

The hillbillies had their own sense of group solidarity. Flint, Michigan, had its "Little Missouri" and "Little Arkansas"

residential settlements. In Akron, the West Virginia State Society had 25,000 members and put on an annual West Virginia day picnic. Marked off from the older inhabitants by their accents, manners and dress, the "snake-eaters" were the butt of ridicule and jokes, which were fiercely resented. A judge in Akron suspended sentence on one man on condition that he return to West Virginia. A newspaper reporter wrote up the incident, "Judge Sentences Man to West Virginia for Life." At the next election the hapless judge was badly beaten by the votes of outraged mountaineers.

The formation of the CIO marked the fusing of the interests of the immigrant and native-stock workers. That, I believe, is perhaps the most telling accomplishment of the CIO. Its political importance can hardly be exaggerated. The mass production industries had been the ones in which racial and religious antagonisms among the workers were most divisive. Carnegie-Illinois, for example, had sprinkled clusters of different nationalities in each of its mines, reasoning correctly that a Balkanized working force would be more difficult to unionize. In some industries immigrants and Negroes had first been introduced as strikebreakers or because they would work for lower wages than native-born workers. The failure of the Knights of Labor in the 1880's was largely a failure to unite the immigrant working groups. Much of the A. F. of L.'s reluctance to embark on a real organizing drive in the mass production industries reflected the dislike of the "aristocrats of labor" in the skilled crafts for the immigrant "rubbish."

By 1935, of course, the immigrants had made considerable progress toward Americanization. But the key to the change was the rise of a common class consciousness among all workers. The depression, in making all workers more aware of their economic interests, suppressed their racial and religious antagonisms. Put crudely, the hatred of bankers among the native American workers had become greater than their hatred of the Pope or even of the Negro. . . .

Negroes were another voting element which was determined to go forward rather than back. In some cities as many as four out of five Negro families were on relief. "Don't Buy Where You Can't Work" campaigns were being pressed to force white storeowners to hire Negroes. In Harlem the accumulated tensions of the depression years were exploded suddenly by a trivial incident.

On March 19, 1935, a sixteen-year-old boy snatched a ten-cent bread knife from a five-and-ten cent counter—"just for fun" he later told the police. Two white clerks and the white manager chased the boy to the rear of the store. When they grabbed him, he bit their hands and broke away.

The boy was a Puerto Rican, yet the rumor spread that a Negro had been lynched in the store. Pickets appeared. A soapbox orator on one street corner attracted a growing crowd. When a funeral hearse happend to drive by a woman shrieked, "They've come to take the boy's body!" The Negro mob went on a rampage. When the riot was over, one man was dead—three others died later of injuries—and a hundred or more whites and Negroes had been shot, stabbed or stoned.

The grisly tragedy was lightened only by the action of a Chinese laundryman. When he saw the mob surging through the streets, heaving stones into store windows, he hastily thrust a sign into his window, "Me colored too."

New York City had had four previous race riots, without anything much happening afterward. The 1935 riot, however, set off a series of far-reaching changes. Harlem's shopowners hastily put on Negro employees. Before the year was out Tammany Hall had named its first Negro district leader. Mayor Fiorello La Guardia had appointed the first Negro magistrate. In 1932 most Negro voters in the country were still Republican. In 1936, in many cities two of every three Negro voters were for Roosevelt.

And so it went all through the country. It would be impossible to trace in full all the different ways in which the question—whether to go back or forward—was being asked of the American people. Sometimes the query was put bluntly in so many words. More often it was implicit in the logic of events or in reminders of the depression. At the end of 1935, more than $780,000,000 was still tied up in closed banks, 3,000,000 persons were still on relief; one survey of a group of garment workers showed that half of them had not bought a new coat for four years.

Lifelong Socialists had to ask themselves—did they return to the ivory tower of a futile third party or did they defend their immediate interests by rallying behind Roosevelt? Sidney Hillman and David Dubinsky, whose unions had been saved by the N.R.A., formed a new American Labor party to enable New Yorkers to vote for Roosevelt and still remain independent of the Democrats. Norman Thomas polled 884,000 Socialist votes nationally in 1932 and only 187,000 votes four years later.

On the other side of the political barricades the realignment was equally sharp. In 1932 one fourth of the Democratic campaign funds was contributed by bankers. In 1936 bankers accounted for a mere 3 per cent of the Democratic party's war chest. (Their total contributions to the Democrats were only about a third of the $750,000 spent by organized labor.)

Particularly in rural areas, the 1936 vote showed that sizable numbers of voters were ready to return to the Republicanism of their ancestors. Winston County, which had seceded from Alabama during the Civil War to remain loyal to the union, swung back to the Republican party in 1936; so did thirty-two counties in Missouri, all but eight bone-dry by tradition. Less than a dozen wheat counties in the whole country had stayed Republican in 1932. Four years later, most of the wheat counties were on their way back to the Republican party.

In the industrial centers, however, the political allegiances that had grown out of the Civil War were uprooted for good. In New York, New Jersey and Pennsylvania, alone, the Democratic vote leaped by roughly 1,800,000. Despite the depression, in 1932, Roosevelt failed to carry a dozen cities with 100,000 or more population—Philadelphia, Scranton and Reading in Pennsylvania; Can-

ton, Youngstown and Columbus in Ohio; Gary, Duluth, Des Moines, Grand Rapids and Springfield, Massachusetts. Every one swung for Roosevelt in 1936 and except for Grand Rapids have remained Democratic since.

A dramatic glimpse into the nature of this hidden political revolution will be found by comparing the 1928 and 1936 vote in our major cities. While Smith won six of every ten voters in some cities, in others he drew only three out of ten. This disparity had narrowed by 1932, but wide divergencies in voting still prevailed in different parts of the country. With the 1936 election, as the table below shows, the voting of nearly all our major cities hit a common level.

Whether the cities are heavily foreign born or native American in make-up, Catholic or Protestant, with large numbers of Negroes or of whites up from the South, did not make too much difference in their 1936 vote. Nor whether the city had a strong labor tradition like San-Francisco or an open shop tradition like Los Angeles, nor whether it was located on the East or West coast or in the Midwest.

Cities High Smith			Cities Low Smith		
City	Dem. % 1928	Dem. % 1936	City	Dem. % 1928	Dem. % 1936
Lawrence	71	73	Flint	19	72
Boston	67	63	Wichita, Kan.	24	64
Lowell	64	61	Los Angeles	28	67
Fall River	64	67	Akron	31	71
New York	60	75	Des Moines	31	55
New Haven	57	65	San Diego	32	65
Milwaukee	53	76	Seattle	32	64
New Bedford	52	65	Duluth	32	71
Cleveland	52	76	Canton	34	66
St. Louis	51	66	Spokane	35	71
San Francisco	49	72	Detroit	37	65
Chicago	48	65	Indianapolis	39	57
Pittsburgh	47	67	Philadelphia	39	60
Baltimore	47	67	Youngstown	39	74

A new nationalizing force had clearly been injected into American politics. In the past American political realignments have always followed sectional lines. The Revolt of the City, however, had drawn the same class-conscious line of economic interest across the entire country, overriding not only regional distinctions but equally strong cultural differences.

This development was not without its irony. In drawing the line of cleavage between the worker and "economic royalist," Roosevelt unquestionably sharpened the sense of class division in American society. Yet, in doing so, he subordinated the old nativistic prejudices of race and religion, which had divided the lower half of American society for so long, bringing these lower income elements a greater degree of social unity than they had ever shared before. Was Roosevelt dividing or unifying the country? . . .

By Fire and Water

If the 1936 vote marked the emergence of the new Roosevelt coalition, the third term election brought the crucial trial by fire and water which demonstrated the coalition's durability.

In both 1932 and 1936 Roosevelt would still have been elected without his heavy urban pluralities. In 1940, however, with the war and the third-term issue cutting heavily into his rural strength, the margin of victory that accounted for at least 212 electoral votes was supplied by the dozen largest cities in the country.

In every city I visited while doing a postelection survey I found that the Roosevelt vote broke at virtually the same economic level, between $45 and $60 a month rent. Below that line his pluralities were overwhelming. Above it, they faded away. In Pittsburgh, for example, Roosevelt got three fourths of the vote in wards whose rentals averaged under $40 a month and only four tenths of the vote where rentals were above $65 a month. Minneapolis, whose social make-up contrasts sharply with Pittsburgh, showed much the same results—about 40 per cent of the vote for Roosevelt in the highest income ward, but seven of every ten voters in the lower rental areas.

The sharpness with which the balloting stratified in city after city—Chicago, Boston, St. Louis, Seattle, Cleveland— left little room for any appreciable shift of votes because of the campaign put on by Wendell Willkie. When I asked one auto unionist in Detroit why the third-term issue had made so little difference he replied, "I'll say it even though it doesn't sound nice. We've grown class conscious." With other unions there may have been less bitterness but the division between worker and "economic royalist" was as sharply drawn. In a Minneapolis ward, inhabited largely by teamsters, the pastor of one church had been outspoken in condemning the third term. He admitted bitterly, "I don't suppose I changed a single vote." John Lewis, who had endorsed Willkie, could have echoed him.

This class consciousness, it should be noted, was not confined to workers. The balloting revealed as much class feeling among the higher income Republicans. If Roosevelt solidified the lower classes, he also welded the upper class.

The one sharp break from "economic voting" came on the basis of ethnic background, reflecting the varying impact upon different groups of Hitler's War. Roosevelt's heaviest losses came in German-American and Italo-American wards, where resentment was strong against his "stab in the back" reference to Mussolini's attack on France. The highest income areas voting for Roosevelt were Jewish. In Brooklyn he carried streets with $15,000 homes—a comfortable valuation in 1940—and apartment houses with doormen. Where low income status coincided with the nationality background of a country invaded by Germany, the vote for Roosevelt was prodigious. Polish-American wards in Buffalo went Democratic nine to one, with individual precincts running as high as twenty to one, his heaviest pluralities in the whole country.

Curiously, the ethnic elements most bitterly antagonized by Hitler were largely those contributing the heaviest numbers of new voters. In Buffalo, in 1940, the Polish-Americans mustered enough votes to elect a Polish-American judge for the first time. One Democratic ward leader, John Kryzinski, a tavern keeper, was foaming with enthusiasm at the significance of this victory.

"Out in ritzy Humboldt Park they get two voters to a family," he snorted contemptuously. "I get six out of my house. I got neighbors who give me eight. We elected a judge this year. The way things are going in eight years we'll elect a mayor."

Nine years later Buffalo did elect Joseph Mruc its first Polish-American mayor.

In every city one could see the same inexorable spread of numbers and the same leveling pressures. Almost it seemed, in fact, that the Republicans had decided to abandon the cities to the Democratic masses, taking refuge in the suburbs. In St. Louis the Twenty-eighth Ward had stayed Republican in 1932. By 1940 this G.O.P. stronghold had been reduced to three precincts. Along Lindell Boulevard and Skinker Road, "For Sale" signs were propped in front of mansionlike homes with graveled driveways, flagstone walks and antique-fabricated lampposts. Some of the more imposing residences were being razed to make way for apartment houses. In the old days at the Pageant, the neighborhood movie house, seats were reserved. When I saw it, the lobby was placarded with handbills advertising double features on Wednesdays and Thursdays, with three features for a quarter on Fridays and Saturdays.

In Harlem, as well, the spirit of 1936 had quickened. Along 125th Street Negroes were working in hundreds of establishments which as late as 1935 had been manned completely by whites. Garment workers, janitors, bartenders, waiters and waitresses, Pullman porters, laundry workers, newspaper men, retail clerks and redcaps were flocking into labor unions with a sense of deliverance. To the Negro, unionism promised more than a wage boost. It also seemed the trumpet which would eventually tumble the Jericho walls of discrimination. Some Harlem unions were holding daily classes to teach Negroes selling, typing and stenography, to be able to rebuff employers who protested, "I can't hire Negroes, they're not experienced."

Probably 50 per cent of Harlem's Negroes were still getting relief of some kind. Older Negroes, clinging to the Republican party, might shake their graying heads and mutter, "Our people are selling their birthrights for a mess of pottage." Younger Negroes had a different slant on WPA. "The really important thing about WPA is that it is a guarantee of a living wage," explained Carl Lawrence, a reporter on the *Amsterdam News*. "It means Negroes don't have to work for anything people want to give them. This helps lift the standards of all Negroes even those not on WPA."

The fall of France in 1940 had spurted the armament program, and the defense boom had been building up steadily in the months before the election. With the boom in employment, a highly significant thing was happening. Older people, who had been thrown out of work during the depression, were not being re-employed. The jobs were going to their children, while the older folk stayed on relief or lived on their savings, plus some help from their children. It hardly had been planned that way, but the New Deal was cushioning a wholesale shift in the working population, by easing the older generation of depression casualties out of the way to make room for a new generation.

In the Charlestown area of Boston one half of the voters were under forty. The ward leader himself, William Galvin, was thirty-six. Two younger brothers had got out of high school during the depression and had gone into the CCC camps. When employment in the Boston Navy Yard expanded, they got jobs as electrician's and pipe fitter's helpers. From the CCC to the Navy Yard—to these two youths, the government had brought advancement as real as any they could have achieved under a private employer.

As a reporter in Washington I had shared the general belief that the New Deal was hastily improvised and animated by no coherent philosophy. When one translated its benefits down to what they meant to the families I was interviewing in 1940, the whole Roosevelt program took on a new consistency.

The depression had thrown grave strains upon lower income families. Many family heads had lost their jobs, never to be employed regularly again. In some instances, the children were old enough to take over the breadwinning, which often robbed the deposed patriarch of his self-respect. In other families the parents had to struggle along until the children grew of age and took over.

In varied ways the New Deal eased these family strains. Through the HOLC a million homes were saved. Many homeowners were too old to have been able to buy a new home, if they had lost their old ones. With the children grown older, I found, many were renting out part of the house, often to a married son or daughter.

Into the CCC camps went 2,750,000 sons of the cities. No longer a drain on the family larder, they even sent some money back home. Children in high school might get NYA aid. Those who went to work usually did so in low-wage industries where the effects of the wage-hour law were most noticeable.

These and other New Deal benefits did not solve all the family problems by any means. They did ease the adjustments that had to be made as the unfortunates of one generation grew unemployable and another generation finally found its opportunity in defense employment.

The recovery from the depression low helped Roosevelt politically with all groups. It was particularly important in the cities because that recovery coincided with the hatching out of the birth rates of 1910 to 1920 and the rise of a new generation. The very size of the Democratically inclined families helped knit them to the New Deal. Even persons who had done rather well for themselves were likely to have a less fortunate family member lower down the economic ladder being benefited by the New Deal. Old-age pensions and other aid eased the burden of having to care for parents too old to work. Instead of being dragged by family burdens, the rising generation was able to solidify its gains. ....

Suggestions for Additional Reading

The selections in this book make up only a fragmentary sampling of the vast literature on the New Deal. Yet we are still so close to the period—in time and in spirit—that studies which look upon it with historical perspective are scarce indeed.

Arthur M. Schlesinger, Jr.'s multivolume *The Age of Roosevelt* is the most substantial New Deal history of our time. So far, *The Crisis of the Old Order, The Coming of the New Deal,* and *The Politics of Upheaval* (Boston, 1957–1960) have appeared, bringing the story down through the 1936 election. This is a perceptive, well-written work, imbued with the author's conviction that the New Deal was an exciting, worthwhile, successful venture.

There are numerous good one-volume studies of the New Deal. Basil Rauch's pioneering *The History of the New Deal* (New York, 1944); Denis W. Brogan, *The Era of Franklin D. Roosevelt* (New Haven, 1950); and Dexter Perkins, *The New Age of Franklin Roosevelt, 1932–45* (Chicago, 1957), see the New Deal as a successful experiment in democratic government. Two interesting contemporary surveys are Arthur M. Schlesinger, Sr., *The New Deal in Action 1933–1939* (New York, 1940), and Louis M. Hacker, *American Problems of Today* (New York, 1939), pp. 177–332. Schlesinger found the New Deal to be "a reassertion and extension of the ideals of the earlier progressive movement"; Hacker termed it "a political program in behalf of agricultural landlords and big commercial farmers, organized trade unionists, and overseas investors and imperialist promoters."

Of the mass of books interpreting the New Deal as an unwise and unnecessary break from tradition, Raymond Moley's *After Seven Years* (New York, 1939), and Edgar E. Robinson's *The Roosevelt Leadership), 1933–1945* (Philadelphia, 1955), stand out.

Eric Goldman's chapters on the New Deal in his *Rendezvous With Destiny: A History of Modern American Reform* (New York, 1952) are a sprightly rendering. Richard Hofstadter has an interesting, though fragmentary, analysis of the New Deal as a break with past traditions of American reform in *The Age of Reform* (New York, 1955).

Frank Freidel is writing a biography of Franklin D. Roosevelt which in lengtn, sweep, and friendly interpretation parallels the junior Schlesinger work. So far, his published volumes only come down to 1932. The best one–volume biography of FDR is James M. Burns, *Roosevelt: the Lion and the Fox* (New York, 1956). Burns emphasizes Roosevelt's ultimate failure to institute substantial political and social reforms. John Gunther's *Roosevelt in Retrospect* (New York, 1950) is an anecdote-filled portrait, and Rexford G. Tugwell, *The Democratic Roosevelt* (Garden City, N. Y., 1957) is a rich combination of interpretation and recollection.

The abundant memoirs of participants in the Roosevelt administrations are major—if often conflicting—sources of information and interpretation. The best of them are Frances Perkins, *The Roosevelt I Knew* (New York, 1946); Eleanor Roosevelt, *This I Remember* (New York, 1949); and Harold Ickes, *The Secret Diary of Harold L. Ickes* (3 vols., New York, 1953–1954).

A related type of book, half memoir and half history, is highly useful; its prevalence speaks eloquently of the still undeveloped state of New Deal historiography. Robert E. Sherwood, *Roosevelt and Hopkins: An Intimate History* (New York, 1948); John M. Blum, *From the Morgenthau Diaries: Years of Crisis, 1928–1938* (Boston, 1959); and Moley's *After Seven Years* are the best of these.

There is a great mass of material on the agencies, policies, and effects of the New Deal. A useful contemporary guide is U.S. Library of Congress, Division of Bibliography, *A Selected List of References on the New Deal* (Washington, D.C., 1940); see also Oscar Handlin *et al., Harvard Guide to American History* (Cambridge, Mass., 1954), pp. 256–264. Frank Freidel, "The New Deal, 1929–1941," *Yearbook of the National Council for the Social Studies*, XXXI (1961), 264–281, is an informed discussion of New Deal materials. See also the extensive critical bibliography in Robinson, *Roosevelt Leadership*, pp. 411–480.